32/- 190

'74

B
796.72

389547

HEADLINE HOCKEY

●●●●●●●●●●●●●●●●●●●●●●●●

HEADLINE HOCKEY

ANDY O'BRIEN

THE RYERSON PRESS TORONTO

Published by *The Ryerson Press, Canada.*
Printed and bound by *The Ryerson Press, Toronto.*

●●●●●●●●●●●●●●●
DEDICATED TO

*The kid on skates who somewhere
in Canada on some long-past day
on some patch of frozen water,
first felt the thrill of juggling
a frozen something at the end of
a hooked stick. What would we
have ever done without him?*

•••••••••••
CONTENTS

Foreword   ix

●●●●●●●●●●●●●●
PHOTOGRAPHS

●●●●●●●●●●●
FOREWORD

It was Saturday night, April 13, 1940, and a chill rain fell on Toronto. The only place drearier than outside the Maple Leaf Gardens was inside.

Leafs had just been knocked out of the Stanley Cup finals by the Rangers from New York, in a sizzling sixth game, 3-2. In the Leafs' dressing-room, where a sign says defeat doesn't rest lightly on the team's shoulders, it didn't. And over in that little oasis of joy, the Rangers' room, an immediate problem of awesome dimension had subdued the jubilation of even the red-blooded Americans who weren't really Americans at all.

It had suddenly dawned on the new hockey champions of the world that the traditional "champagne victory party" would be held in New York—not tonight in Toronto where they were in effect marooned. Mindful of possible overtime delays, Rangers had been booked out on the next morning's train.

But what about tonight?

In the Toronto of 1940 there weren't many, if any, places to fête even the thrill of a lifetime, and all with the bewitching hour of midnight approaching on a Saturday night!

Manager Lester Patrick called a summit meeting of Ranger executive and, out of solemn conclave, came the decision to stage "a small and exclusive interim party limited to not more than thirty-five players, press and executive" in a private salon at the Royal York Hotel. A delegate was rushed away pronto. Patrick was well-schooled and able; by the time the victors had showered and taxied downtown, toting the Stanley Cup, he had a festive board and generous bar set up and operational. Everybody co-operated with exuberant enthusiasm and, in nothing flat, joy was unconfined.

Then the roof fell in.

Near the private salon there was a ballroom where a major dance was shuffling into its final gasp. Suddenly word flashed that a Stanley Cup party was underway next door. With whoop and holler, gay guys and gals stormed the Ranger portals where they were vigorously greeted by the refugees from a monastic playoff life. The salon took on a Times Square look and zoomed into high gear.

On the sober, silent, sombre Sunday morrow, just before train time, Manager Patrick was handed the bill—and a glass of cold water. The small and exclusive party had cost $3,700.

I related this incident to John Webster Grant, Editor of The Ryerson Press, Toronto. He had just invited me to write an "informal" history of headline hockey. By informal, he explained, was meant something brief and breezy.

"Brief?" I exploded. "How could I, how could anybody, write a brief history of hockey in the headline strata? Since the inception of the National Hockey League in 1917, enough thunderous things have happened to fill an opus taller than you. In Olympic and international hockey, too, so many great players, coaches and builders have come and gone. So many incidents have to be told such as . . . ." (Here I injected the one above).

But Editor Grant remained adamant. When I paused for air, he injected: "My idea of a happy book is one I'd buy at the Montreal airport. It would both inform and relax me until it and the flight came to an end on the runway at Winnipeg."

"Sufferin' cats!" I said, or the equivalent thereof, "are you flying in a DC 8?"

He nodded. That meant about three and one-half hours flying time with a few minutes out for a meal. It would sure call for a lot of history-hacking, but the thought dawned on me that the history of World War II could be told simply by retelling the story of Winston Churchill. Nor would it be necessary to tell all the anecdotes or all the deeds associated with him. What's more, all of us who served in any way in World War II would feel a "sharing" just in reading the story of the man whose spirit dominated the war's history. So it could be that all who helped make hockey great on or off the ice should feel a sharing in even an informal history of their game — whether or not they or their deeds are mentioned.

Editor Grant shoved a contract across the desk. "Well, will you pilot the plane, captain?"

I reached for my pen.

On behalf of the crew I welcome you aboard this flight into the wonderful, wacky world of headline hockey I've known for thirty-one press-box years. Please fasten your belts in preparation for take-off.

ANDY O'BRIEN

●●●●●●●●●●●●●
CHAPTER ONE

Those Incredible Vees from Penticton, B.C.

THE YEAR: *1955.*

SCENE: *Cologne, Germany.*

EVENT: *Canada versus Poland in the World Hockey Tournament.*

Canada's Bill Warwick and Poland's Stanislaus Bacilek had drawn a penalty for a violent exchange of shoving. As they sat down in the sinbin, Bacilek asked in flawless English: "Why don't you play fair?"

Warwick was astonished. "You speak better English than I do but I'm glad. You will understand when I say that unless you quit holding me I will flatten your pointed head."

Into the atmosphere of delicate diplomacy which stressed the international goodwill that West Germany had cautiously created in 1955, plunged the Gashouse Gang from the Okanagan Valley.

It seemed they could do nothing right—except win games.

As rugged as the Rockies, as raw as the winter that swept down from those thunderous hills, were the Penticton Vees. *Time Magazine* deplored that in winning back the world title from Russia the Vees' behaviour "both on and off the ice was anything but ambassadorial." After what had been billed as a friendly, pre-tourney exhibition game in Czechoslovakia, the *Communist Daily Worker* of London reported:

The name of Canadian ice hockey stinks in Czecho-slovakia after last night's game in which the Penticton

1

Vees battered, slashed and punched their way to a
3-3 draw with the Czechoslovakian national side ...
the thousands of people who were stunned by the
thuggery on ice in the end rightly booed them off the
ice.

As for the Vees, they were no less critical of themselves.

The night they shattered the German team, 10-1, player-
coach Grant Warwick tore a strip off his collective team for
playing "a lousy game" and ordered a practice next morning
in Düsseldorf, although their tourney grind had them playing
eight games in ten nights in four cities. There were loud mutters
of protest in the dressing-room. Forward Jack McIntyre
abruptly turned to me and asked:

"Did we really look that bad out there tonight?"

A sudden silence fell as coach and players glared at me reflec-
tively. There was no place to hide, and I couldn't think of a
plausible fib on the spur of the moment. So I simply said:
"Yes."

To my utter astonishment everybody nodded understand-
ingly. McIntyre tugged off a skate, threw it on the floor and
sighed:

"We never look good but the score does. You should have
seen how awful we looked last year when we won the Allan Cup."

Rough and tough and born to turbulence—that they were.
But never before or since has a Hockey Adventure so captivated the Canadian public. And after the furious fever of those
madcap days and nights with the Vees had abated, I found I'd
learned more about hockey from them than from years following National Hockey League teams.

To explain why, I have to take you back a bit—to Berlin
where I paused, all alone, for what was intended to be a
refreshing pause en route to the tourney doings in Düsseldorf,
Cologne, Krefeld and Dortmund.

At the Pan American Airways headquarters, I talked a handsome young ex-Luftwaffe pilot into "smuggling" me into East Berlin for a looksee at Communist domination in action, plus the bunker in which Adolf Hitler had done Germany its biggest favour.

He drove me in his wee car. At the Brandenburg Gate he told me to light up a large cigar and simply smile broadly when anybody looked at me. He stepped out and spoke for some time to the armed Commies who finally waved us through. He explained that I was now "an American capitalist who was thinking of investing some money in East Berlin."

While standing outside the barbed wire that now surrounds the suicide scene of Adolf, a jeep with two armed soldiers ripped up just as my escort was shooting a souvenir picture. I lighted a fresh cigar, beamed at the sombre soldiers and, once again, got by.

Two hours of East Berlin was enough. After being awed by West Berlin's booming revival and the neon-lighted Kurfür-stendamm, the still bomb-blasted setting of the East sector and its shuffling, furtive-looking, shabbily dressed citizens, I felt a bit nauseated. We returned, without incident, to the Hotel Kempinski and sat down over an American bourbon—or two.

My German escort left me with: "Now you know why it's important to us of West Berlin that the Russians get stopped in everything they try . . . and while, to you from Canada, it may be only a bunch of hockey games coming up, to us of West Berlin, surrounded by the Communists, it will be a boost for morale every time they are beaten. You people call it a cold war," here he obviously strained in German fashion to be jocular, "but what better place is there to fight it than on ice, ja?"

Left alone in Berlin, with three ice cubes and a glass, it dawned on me what pressure had been placed on this team from far-off British Columbia.

Back in Canada the Vees had been led to believe it was purely a matter of hockey revenge. The 1954 tournament, held in Stockholm, had seen Russia enter a team for the first time and win it—beating Canada en route, 7-2. It was Vees' task to re-establish supremacy in the game Canada regarded as her birthright.

But, in the period of the massive flight from their compact Penticton (population 11,894) almost overnight into the age-old atmosphere of the Continent, the Vees found their mission was much more than mere hockey.

Certainly the hockey chore ahead was stern enough. They would have to ride roughshod over teams representing the United States, Czechoslovakia, Poland, Sweden, Switzerland, Germany and Finland because the powerful Russian team certainly would. In case of a tie in points between two teams at the top, the Cup would go to the team with the most goals scored. So the Vees skated into the tourney with one single, blazing aim—to win 'em all by thumping big scores up to the final game with Russia, and then beat the Reds, too. But something new had been added.

In the pre-tourney game in Czechoslovakia where, according to the *Daily Worker*, they had been booed off the ice, the team from the Okanagan Valley had been awed by fans "just wanting to touch our coats and sweaters." They had handed out everything they could give as souvenirs and been thanked by tear-filled eyes. On every side they were furtively slipped letters to mail to relatives outside the Red Curtain.

From that moment losing became unthinkable for the Vees. Their attitude was far removed from ye olde "matters not who wins but how you play the game." I don't ask you to approve of it, I just want you to appreciate the setting into which they skated.

Yet, they managed to combine frolic with fury.

There was the hilarious episode during the Canada versus

4

Switzerland game. Normally the three Warwick brothers formed the Vees' big line—Dick at centre, flanked by Bill and Grant. But, during this game, with the Canadian lead piled up, Grant, as coach, replaced himself with Jack McIntyre. It resulted in the most teeth-rattling bodycheck of the entire tournament when, unaccustomed to one another, the two wings collided at mid-ice.

It was more than just a high-speed collision. Bill's reflexes, long schooled in survival-of-the-fittest Western hockey, automatically whipped a mallet-like elbow into McIntyre's jaw at the split-second of contact. Down went McIntyre, and the referee, also registering automatically, blew his whistle. While the ref was puzzling over the problem of how to penalize a player for dropping one of his team mates, McIntyre rolled over on the ice, sat up dazedly and, while the movie cameras focused for a close-up on his face, he peeled off an obvious and all-comprehensive criticism of Bill's ancestry.

While the cameramen were pawing wildly for their "stop" switches, the German fans broke into gales of laughter. Afterwards in the dressing-room, Dick added his own comment for the press: "They deserved it. Both of them have been trying to be centremen all season."

Both Grant and Bill had made the National Hockey League; in fact, Grant was rookie of the year in 1941/42. He was then playing with New York Rangers, later saw service with Boston Bruins and Montreal Canadiens. Bill spent two years with Rangers; a shattering auto accident had supposedly ended his ice career. Dick never deserted amateur ranks despite several bids.

The three brothers opened a restaurant in Penticton. They returned to hockey with the local Vees "just to keep in shape."

Playing hockey the only way they knew how, a game at a time, 1954 found them—to their own amazement—not only winners of the Allan Cup, emblematic of what Canada win-

5

somely labels its senior amateur championship, but also automatic crusaders to redeem the nation's prestige internationally in 1955.

Reinstated pros are eligible in world tournament hockey, although not in the Olympics. The broader "world" outlook asks only that the players not have hockey as their major source of livelihood. The Russian national team is actually more pro than our N.H.L. players because they work at hockey eleven months of the year. In the Communist programme for world domination, this is their contribution, and they get around even the Olympic oath by being officially members of the Red Army.

The seasoned experience of the Warwicks slowly won over the German fandom in the 1955 tourney. At first the fans saw only the team's love of harsh, bodily contact play. One night, against the Finns, Bill bowled over a defenceman in the first few minutes, and when the other Finn defenceman rushed up to say something, Bill dropped him, too, with an elbow on the jaw.

When Bill ran into a scathing bawling-out from brother Grant for drawing the penalty, he pleaded that he was about to be attacked by the second Finn. Grant loudly pointed out the second Finn was merely protesting politely.

"Hell, Grant," replied Bill, "I can't speak Finn and, anyway, why should I be nice to these Commies?"

The discussion took a detour. Somebody said the Finns weren't Commies at all. Milt Dunnell of the *Toronto Daily Star* was called in and confirmed they weren't. Bill was genuinely penitent.

It prompted the incomparable Len Norris of the *Vancouver Sun* to do a cartoon that was published gleefully in England as well as throughout North America. It showed Bill standing with a broken stick, amid fallen ice foes and surrounded by booing fans, while giving an interview to a German reporter. The caption under the cartoon reads: ". . . and if, through the medium of this great sport, we have contributed to the betterment of international relations and understanding, then we are indeed amply rewarded. . . ."

But the game against Germany in Düsseldorf, despite Vees' 10-1 victory, won a lot of German fans for Vees. The tough German defence learned to bodycheck and really handed it out in the first period. They dropped the Vees' attackers repeatedly but, the fans noted, clean checks never provoked retaliation. The fallen Vees popped up pronto, without any of the "dying swan" routines the Russians used to impress the referee. It dawned on the fans that the Vees could take it as well as hand it out.

Again, they were impressed by an incident at the end of the Canada-Finland game. As the final klaxon sounded, the Vees on the bench poured over the boards and joined those on the ice in rushing at the Finn goalie, young Lars Svensson. For a moment Lars poised for flight, then he was surrounded by Vees shaking his hand, clapping him on the back. Lars had let in twelve but he had stopped over fifty shots, and the Vees rushed to congratulate him before congratulating one another.

The same fans were frankly puzzled at Dortmund when the Vees swamped the United States' team, 12-1. Some six hundred Canadian troops had come over from the camp at Soest and booed the Yanks relentlessly, bellowing: "Go home and learn hockey!" I suppose the Germans expected American and Canadians to be brothers under the skin—uneasily they seemed to suspect this was a severing of western unity.

By the third period, however, their education had progressed to the point where some German fans among the Canadian troops were booing the Vees and even entering into good-natured debate featuring broken English and broken German.

Meanwhile, in the press box, we from Canada were being educated, too.

For some years I've suspected that N.H.L. players are getting over-coached. The parent team trains its coaches in minor pro and amateur sponsored clubs to follow a set pattern. They all stress positional hockey; players mainly stay in their allotted lanes, skate fast and faster, repeat their own pet tricks and depend on the percentage in clicking. Defencemen also follow a pattern. The result is such a sameness that all N.H.L. teams look alike, and the players are so alike that one can shift to another team and almost overnight look as if he always wore the new sweater.

The only real difference is that in some positions some teams have better craftsmen than others. But when they face something "different," too often the patterned players are stymied—until they and their coaches work out a new technique in practice.

Canadiens loaned Bobby Rousseau, then the top amateur in Canada, to the Canadian Olympic team at Squaw Valley in 1960. He was a major disappointment; he looked helpless. He told me: "They play awfully different hockey; everybody goes for the puck and I was left with no clear ice. I was frustrated." Yet, in 1961/62 Rousseau swept the voting as N.H.L. rookie of the year with 144 out of a possible 180 votes.

However, the Vees faced neither patterned teams nor "alike" players. They met, and had to beat, each new team in every tournament game because there would be no second chance and a single loss—even a tie—would have cost them the World Cup. The Vees adjusted to new problems as they met them.

Only the Yanks and Poles were routinely poor. The Czechs were scrappy and skilled; Vees had to fight for their lives and come from behind to win, 3-2. The Germans threw hard body-checks. The Swiss stressed speed, as did the Finns. The Swedes were strong defensively and broke like scared rabbits on break-aways. Yet the Vees, with only Russia to meet, had beaten all other seven nations, piling up sixty goals as compared with only six against.

Goalie Ivan McLelland, a native of Timmins, Ontario, admitted the Vees had a set formula to meet the varying types of opposing teams. He told me: "Whenever we get stymied by a team that seems smarter or stronger or fresher, we just drift the puck in there and keep hammering. They can't score while the puck is in their end, and sometimes we even put it in their net. If we try high-strategy hockey, we only get all fouled up."

The Russians had also won all of their games to date—they didn't have as many goals "for," only 39, but they had almost as few "against," 7.

The pressure build-up for the Sunday final was more intensive than I've ever met in Stanley Cup, Grey Cup or world heavyweight fight super-situations. In the Saturday lull before the payoff game on Sunday afternoon, the press-radio-television representation had swollen to 350 and included Sweden, Poland, Finland, Switzerland, England, the United States, Holland, Belgium, France, Italy, Austria and Germany—as well, of course, as Russia and Canada.

After the Saturday practice, there was violent banging on the dressing-room door at Krefeld. Somebody opened the door a crack, listened, then yelled into the room: "Hey, Grant, *Life Magazine* is outside and wants in. . . ."

Grant Warwick stormed at him: "Keep those picture-hungry guys out of here! Don't let anybody in except Canadians."

A voice suggested that it might be in the best interests of international relations that *Life* be allowed in, too.

"Nuts!" ruled Grant, "We'll win this thing tomorrow and be nice afterwards."

Dick Warwick sighed out loud: "There goes a million dollars worth of free publicity for our restaurant in Penticton right down the drain. I'll bet that when we win the World Cup Grant won't like the handles on it."

Of course, *Life Magazine* shouldn't have felt really bad about the incident. There had been a nasty, national storm aroused

9

by Manager Clem Bird turning down a reception by the Canadian Embassy thrown in the Vees' honour over at Bonn.

Time Magazine reported Clem as replying: "Just a lot of cheese squares—we got better things to do."

In an effort to smooth out the crisis I had Clem Bird up to my room in Düsseldorf's Breidenbacher Hof.

"I'm only a locomotive engineer back home," he said. "I drive it seventy-five miles down the Okanagan and seventy-five miles back. I don't know anything about this international diplomacy razmataz. I thought we were sent over to beat the Russians, not cheese squares."

I sat back and grinned. Phooey on the unnamed External Affairs officer in Ottawa who had been quoted exclaiming: "Such incredibly stupid and silly behaviour!"

Clem Bird was telling me about a pleasant interlude he had in Berlin. Heinz Henschel, a director of the tourney, invited Clem to his home and threw a dinner complete with "fancy candles."

"I wrote a letter home to my wife in the Okanagan," said Clem, "and told her I had no money at the time to buy flowers for the Henschels, even if I had known where to find a flower shop. But I did follow an old Canadian custom and left my rubbers there."

Over five hundred cables poured in from Canada. The one that came closest to raising a collective lump in the Vees' throats was one that didn't even wish them good luck against Russia. It read: "GOD BLESS STOP HURRY HOME."

It was signed: "THE LIQUOR STORE GANG IN PENTICTON."

Going into Sunday the odds were 3-2 that the Reds would win. Waiters in the Breidenbacher Hof kept bugging me for "inside info," and when I kept telling them the Vees would win by three goals, they would gaze at me in stunned disbelief. So accustomed were they to living in trembling awe of the Russian bear's growls, they just couldn't believe it could be chained.

The Vees weren't at all awed.

They had given the Russians a lot of scouting attention and came to the conclusion that it was a good, fast, well-conditioned team but built around one star, Lieutenant-Colonel Weswold Bobrov. A big, tall man, not unlike Gordie Howe in looks and style, he was the Rocket Richard of Russia and their top-scoring ace. He carried himself with astonishing arrogance, protesting loudly to referees and bawling out his mates on the ice in plain sight of the crowd.

Long before game time at Krefeld, thousands were left milling outside the rink, unable to get in. I got to the press box one and one-half hours ahead of game time and ended standing on a bench with Foster Hewitt sitting between my legs talking into a microphone. Even that close I couldn't hear a word, so great was the din as the game got underway.

Within minutes in the Vees' half of the ice, Grant Warwick caught Bobrov with his head down and the Russian star crashed heavily. It was a clean check, no penalty. Bobrov got up slowly. Later, Bobrov tried to kick Doug Kilburn in a mêlée, and Kilburn draped him over the boards, drawing a penalty. Two minutes later Bobrov was skating for a loose puck but pulled up as he saw Kilburn racing from the sin-bin. George McAvoy then threw another clean check, Bobrov sat down on the ice and waved at the referee. McAvoy stood above Bobrov and waved at him.

The German crowd began to laugh and Bobrov blew. With him blew the Russian team. Vees won, 5-0.

Across Canada, we later learned, the entire nation was glued to the radio as Foster Hewitt, wrestling valiantly with a severe cold and four-syllable Russian names, barked play-by-play tidings of triumph over the network.

Because of the time differential, the game had cut into Sunday morning church times in western Canada and score bulletins were given from pulpits. One excited Vancouver cleric was reported as interrupting the service to announce the 5-0 final count.

In Penticton the wee city went completely haywire. Sunday or no Sunday, they opened the bistros. They snake-danced on the streets all day long. The next day saw the House Speaker on Parliament Hill, Ottawa, put off serious business to extol the Vees.

Meanwhile, back at the ranch in Düsseldorf, we had found it's not for nothing that Rhine rhymes with wine. All night along the Allee Strasse it was a moot point which flowed more freely. The Germans, through this Gashouse Gang from the Okanagan, were breathing deeply and joyously again—they had found there were people in the world who could beat the Russians and make them look more like pouting children than swaggering threats. It had been more than a game, indeed.

On Tuesday afternoon, the badly hung-over Vees were picked up by army buses from the First Canadian Infantry Brigade at Soest for two games against all-star army teams. A special escort section of the Provost Company picked them up as they left the autobahn. Behind the four white motorcycles came a jeep equipped wth fire-engine siren, purple blinker light and checkered flag mounted on the hood.

The exultant German press had urged a half holiday for school kids along the way, and the team whirled through huge, cheering crowds in Dortmund, Iserlohn, Hemer and Derlinghofen.

Vees banged their way to two wins over the army all-stars, then went to Zweibrucken for a game against an all-star R.C.A.F. team that almost ended in a free-for-all. It was Grant Warwick himself who halted the mayhem by holding up his hands and yelling:

"Who-in-hell are supposed to be the world champs here?"

The Vees won again. Peace was uproariously restored, and the messes stayed open late.

12

For some time after my return to Canada, I met people who shook heads over the "bad impression" made by the madcap Vees from Penticton in 1955. Eventually I gave up arguing that hockey is like that. It's no pantywaist game; rather it's by nature violent, a 30 m.p.h. skating sport with padded men and sticks and bodily contact permissible. I tried to stress that losing to a rough but capable team arouses fan anger today but that tomorrow it changes to admiration.

After December of 1959 I didn't have to argue any more.

The Polish Ice Federation and the Club Gornik sent an invitation to the three Warwicks, now retired "for keeps" and running a busy restaurant in Edmonton, to come to Warsaw as guests and hold hockey clinics. The invitation read: "We still call you world champions here."

Actually the Poles unknowingly had some technical backing for their claim. The Warwicks kept the real World Cup and sent over a duplicate for the next World Tourney. In April, 1963, while visiting Edmonton, I dropped into the Penalty Box—bar of the new Warwick Restaurant. There stood the trophy, but I refused to believe it was the original. Bill Warwick promptly summoned Leo Ayotte, commissioner of oaths in Edmonton, and signed a sworn statement that it was the original trophy—that the one then held so proudly by Russia was a phony. Bill added that he was beginning to feel a little bad about it, and if the Kremlin would pay his way, he'd lug the real trophy over there personally.

The Warwicks left the restaurant like astronauts at Cape Canaveral. They were met by cheering thousands and presented with flowers by pretty little Polish girls.

The Warwicks went all the way. Not only did they hold hockey clinics, but they donned their old gear and battered sweaters emblazoned with "Canada" on the front and played with Club Gornik in three games. They starred in tying a team from Czechoslovakia and in two wins against a team from Sweden. In the fourth game, at Bydgoszcz, they lined up with

13

a team of eighteen-year-olds against Gornik and got beaten, 9-3, but the Warwicks scored all three—leaving the ice in a veritable cloudburst of cheering.

At Katowice a farewell party on ice was held. The Warwicks donned their playing outfits and supervised a race for a sweater donated by the Montreal Canadiens. They presented a set of goalkeeping equipment from the New York Rangers to their host club. They gave autographs.

In the dressing-room they found the poor Poles staring at their gear. The Warwicks began giving it out, piece by piece. Dick Warwick recalls: "Finally we were down to our rather gamey underwear, and there were guys staring enviously at that. Under Red rule one can't afford underwear just for sport. So we peeled off the underwear, handed that away, too, and were left in our bare pelts."

They dressed in their street clothes and were waving their way through the cheering lines of people, when a smartly dressed, well-groomed young man put his hand on Bill Warwick's sleeve and said in flawless English: "Remember me, Bill?"

Bill stared thoughtfully: "You sure look familiar but where. . . ."

The Polish fellow laughed. "My name is Stanislaus Bacilek. In the penalty box in 1955 you threatened to flatten my pointed head. . . ."

Bill howled in glee, shook hands warmly with Bacilek, stepped back, looked him up and down and commented: "You seem to be doing plenty good for yourself, Stanislaus. You're the best dressed guy I've met in Poland."

"I owe it all to you, Bill" said Bacilek. Then, as Warwick looked puzzled, he continued: "You undoubtedly forgot that when the game ended you shook hands and presented your stick to me. Well, I took it to a friend who duplicated the stick, and it is now a best seller in Poland under the trade name 'Model Canada'."

●●●●●●●●●●●●●●
CHAPTER TWO

Have Hockey Stick,
Will Travel

We were sipping Italian chicory coffee that could curl the hair on an African chacma. Around us in the Majestic Miramonti at Cortina d'Ampezzo sounded the multi-language chatter of the 1956 Winter Olympics.

"You are possibly unaware," said Dr. Joser Gruss, the International Olympic Committee delegate from Czechoslovakia, "that I owe my present career as an obstetrician in Czechoslovakia to the hockey players of Canada."

"How come?" I asked.

"Back in 1924," he mused, "Canada sent over a great team from Toronto to the Olympics. We played them a game which Canada won by 30 goals. That is why I turned to a career in medicine. Up until then, I had been recognized as the greatest goalkeeper in all of Czechoslovkia."

The "road trip" is the very pulse of hockey. Actually, the long trek of the Penticton Vees was only an extension of the incomparable thrill every hockey kid feels on his first trip to a strange and hostile rink across town or in the next town. It varies only in degree.

On a strange, new rink, all foes look formidable. Just as opposing men of the National Hockey League later looked upon Howie Young and Lou Fontinato as bashingest of the badmen in the Big Time, opposing juniors used to look upon Young with the Hamilton Cubs and Fontinato with Guelph Biltmores. But even they could be beaten.

15

Today as yesterday, the challenge of formidable foes and their ribald rooters stirs the red-bloodedness in hockey hearts. The game allows more than speed and science—it's legal to throw teeth-rattling bodychecks that slow down and upset the foe.

To the fans in the stands, there is no thrill to touch the beating of the unbeatable. There is no greater let-down than seeing their unbeatables beaten. And when a Canadian team goes on the long trek across oceans, the sport pages, home radios and televisions become rinks in which millions of fans share the pulse of hockey with their players.

Just as the Vees' long trek to Germany in 1955 headlined its way into Canadian hearts so, a half-century before, did their forefathers captivate the nation.

In January, 1905, a grab-bag team of never-wases and fairly goods, gathered from the ranks of adventurers who had gone in search of Klondike gold, made an awesome, 4,400-mile trek from Dawson City to challenge Ottawa's mighty Silver Seven for the Stanley Cup.

The years have either enhanced or detracted from many details of the trek which so profoundly affected the course of hockey. I travelled to Ottawa to research it "fresh" from the yellowing files of the *Ottawa Citizen* of 1905.

In bits and pieces the drama unfolded from news stories appearing amid such advertisements as those of the T. Lindsay Ltd.: "Perhaps He Needs A New Suit! Special Lines of $6, $7, $10 and $15." And also: "Drunkenness Cured . . . Free Package!"

The more I dug into the story the more astonishing it became. For example, I found myself wondering what a modern N.H.L. team en route to Stanley Cup action would say if asked to train with a skipping rope in the smoking section of a railway car?

Four of the Klondikers "mushed" on dog sleighs from

16

Dawson to Whitehorse. Four others took advantage of a mid-December thaw to make it by bicycle and stage coach. They went on to Skagway, just ahead of a 54-below cold wave which tied them up for five days, during which they had only one practice "on a rink 40 by 50 feet, half of it covered by sand that dulled our skates."

Some had trouble with their feet, blistered as they walked forty miles or more per day, as well as being swollen by frostbite. But finally they sailed aboard the S.S. *Dolphin*, bound for Seattle, the cheers of sourdoughs of the Gold Rush of '97 wishing them well. At Seattle they took a C.P.R. train to Vancouver where another thunderous station-platform ovation awaited them. A press story, filed en route from Field, British Columbia, reported:

> The only accommodation afforded us on the train for training purposes is the smoking-room with a floor eight-feet square. Exclusive rights have been granted us in this respect on account of the passengers being few and no smokers among them. Skipping is the principal exercise indulged in, and owing to two not being able to conveniently train at one time, the quarters are in use most of the day.

At every train stop western well-wishers interrupted what training or sleeping was going on, but at Winnipeg the joyous journey received a jolt with word from Ottawa that, despite the unforeseen delay at Skagway, the Silver Seven positively refused the Klondikers' request to postpone the start of the best-of-three series. Weldy Young, in charge of the Klondikers, roared: "We'll default the first game and take care of the blankety-blank champs in the other two."

They arrived in Ottawa on January 12, 1905. It had taken them twenty-three days by foot, by sea and rail to make a trip that now takes no more than ten hours by air.

The series was scheduled to open the next night—and it did. The default threat evaporated in the heat of Bytown hospitality that included posh quarters at the Russell Hotel, memberships in the Ontario Amateur Athletic Club and blithesome beakers (with free lunch) in Sam Cassidy's sporty club. Cutters pulled by ponies were provided.

Legend says the Klondikers laid lavish bets on themselves—with gold nuggets. While researching the story I interviewed D'Arcy Finn who was the sports editor of the *Ottawa Citizen* at the time.

"I heard a lot about big bets but regarded it as mainly talk," he said. "Frankly, I can't recall any of the fellows looking as if they'd struck it rich. Most of the cost of their long journey had been defrayed by a prospector named Colonel Joe Boyle, and I got the idea the lads were really 'coming out' anyway."

The Klondikers included: a seventeen-year-old goalie (youngest in Stanley Cup history); Albert Forest of Three Rivers, Quebec; Dr. Randy McLellan, Cornwall, Ontario; Jim Johnstone, Ottawa; Norm Watt, Aylmer, Quebec; Hector Smith and George Kennedy, West Selkirk, Manitoba; Dave Fairbairn, Portage la Prairie, Manitoba, and A. N. Martin, Ottawa. They picked up an ex-Yukoner, Lorne Hannay, while passing through Brandon, Manitoba.

In the Silver Seven, the reigning champions of the hockey world, the Klondikers faced the great Frank McGee, Harry Westwick, Larry Gilmour, Harvey Pulford, Alf Smith, Dave Finnie and Fred White.

The first game at Dey's Gladstone Avenue Rink is classed as "the first of the hysterical Cup playoffs" with surging crowds breaking down store windows and police reserves being called out to get the Governor-General, Earl Grey, and parliamentary bigwigs into the game. The Klondikers certainly were a colourful looking lot as they skated out in uniforms described as "black and gold stripes with white knickers and striped stockings."

However, the colour ended there.

The Silver Seven won, 9-2, in what was described as a drab game: "The visitors were clearly outclassed, and while it is true they hardly had time to get in shape, the form they did show was of the most mediocre kind."

Between that game and the next, the cocky Klondikers committed a grave strategic error. They sneered aloud at Frank McGee who had scored only one of the nine goals and predicted that its "heavy" forward line (it really averaged only 164 pounds) planned to "rip up the Ottawas."

The fans turned from benevolent to bellicose. There had been just enough rough stuff in the opener to hint of impending events. Watt had carved an Ottawa player for five stitches and engaged another in a ten-minute brawl.

The hands-across-the-country in the friendly strife of sport stuff evaporated in the second game. The Klondikers got creamed.

From the opening whistle, the Silver Seven's No. 1 bumping target was Watt who soon couldn't tell the difference between a rink light and a Northern Light. In goal, poor young Forest thought he was caught in a revolving door as McGee racked up a total of 14 goals—four of them in 100 seconds. The final score was 23-2 for Ottawa, but the contribution to hockey from the Klondike had one consolation: the beating they took is still the worst ever absorbed in the all-time records of Stanley Cup play.

The dramatic trek melted into "yesterday's story."

Some years ago, at a sports dinner in Ottawa, an old-time newspaperman who had travelled part of the Gold Rush trail in '97 on assignment and been carried away with the he-man tradition of conquering the unconquerable, told me he had been convinced the Klondike team would win. In anticipation of a quick-killing, he had written and published at his own expense a pamphlet with a heading (as I recall it): *The*

Klondikers of 1905—Greatest Hockey Team of All Time. It was to sell for ten cents.

Politely, I replied: "Most interesting—I'd like to have one."

"One?" he barked back at me, "I've got 5,000 of them!"

But it hadn't all been in vain. Canadian hockey fans' imagination had been so stirred by the east-west angle that when the Pacific Coast League came into being, their appetites' were whetted for a test of strength. It finally came eight years later from Victoria, British Columbia, where the Cougars, led by their playing-coach, Lester Patrick, formally challenged the Quebec Bull Dogs to come west and bring their Stanley Cup with them.

The reigning championship Bull Dogs went west—but without the Cup. The star-studded Quebec team (including three future members of the Hockey Hall of Fame in Joe Malone, Joe Hall and Paddy Moran) refused to recognize the western opposition as calibre worthy of Cup competition.

"Okay," shrugged Patrick, "let's make it an exhibition series —come anyway and see if you can beat us."

The Bull Dogs took a decisive shellacking. They lost two of the three-game series, were out-scored 16-12. Thoroughly cowed, they slunk back through the Rockies with the triumphant yips of the west haunting their dreams.

That was 1913, but the fat was in the fire—the 1914 challenge of Victoria couldn't be ignored. The Cougars came east and lost, but the following year, 1915, the Cup travelled west with the Ottawas to be claimed in resounding style by the great Vancouver Millionaires who featured no less than six future members of the Hall of Fame: "Cyclone" Taylor, Frank Nighbor, Si Griffis, Mickey MacKay, Hughie Lehman and playing-manager Frank Patrick. The Vancouver team swept all three games, out-scoring the east, 26-9. This zoomed the annual trek into the same exalted status football's Grey Cup classic now enjoys with national fandom.

Backstage on the treks there was a rollicking tang of adven-

Rocket Richard, unconscious shortly before, returned to score epic playoff goal through entire Boston team in 1952. Boston goalie Jim Henry, nose broken and two black eyes, shakes his hand.

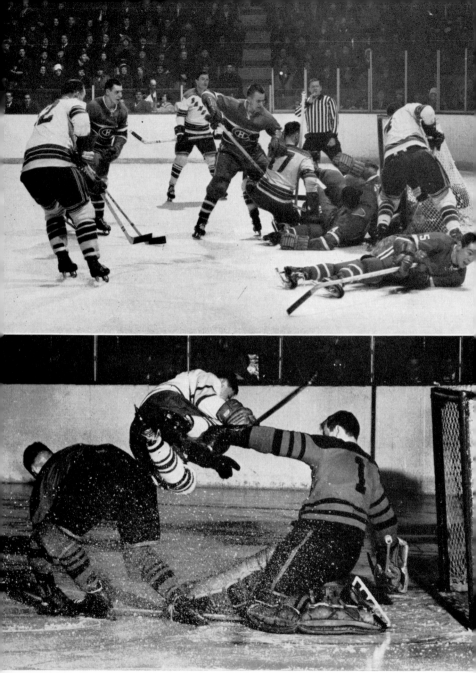

David Bier Studios   Alexandra Stud[

The National Hockey League plays it all-out. Above is a typical, furious pile-up in front of Rangers' net during game with Canadiens.

They go all-out at junior level as well. This prize photo was caught as Marlies' Wally Bayer went into orbit at Maple Leaf Gardens.

ture we don't—for better or for worse—find in Stanley Cup dramas of today.

The late Sprague Cleghorn (also a Hall of Famer) was a star of the Canadiens who went west to defend their title against Victoria Cougars in 1925. It was the last east-to-west trek. A violent fellow on the defence, Sprague liked explosive fun off the ice as well. He and the immortal Howie Morenz (then a rookie) used to amuse themselves in Montreal by carrying cannon firecrackers while driving around Montreal and dropping them under police cars in traffic jams. They'd howl in glee when the cops came tumbling out of each side of the patrol car drawing revolvers.

But the Canadiens could do no wrong in Montreal. When they boarded the train for the west, well-wishers loaded their special car with cases of gin and brandy plus seventy-eight quarts of beer. Sprague told me the supply didn't last beyond Fort William, Ontario.

Morenz, who had never been farther west than Stratford, Ontario, was told that the clock advanced one hour at main divisional points. Every time the train stopped for a fairly lengthy period, Sprague would tell Morenz it was a main divisional point.

"By the time we got to Vancouver," Sprague related, "Howie was ahead a full day. But he was also ahead $500 in poker."

Canadiens lost the Cup in Victoria, but it didn't depress them for long. Players in Stanley Cup playoffs of that era were paid off in cash—young Morenz now had a roll to choke the proverbial cow and followed Sprague's advice: "Don't remove your pants until you get back to Montreal."

The trek ended in a flourish. The gay Canadiens had their special car detached from the transcontinental train at Banff and run off onto a siding. This was a base for a party that left echoes rattling around the Big Hills for a week.

And, already, hockey had developed an international thrill flavour for Canadians.

In 1920 ice hockey appeared for the first time in the Winter Olympics at the Ice Palace in Antwerp, Belgium. Canada sent over the Winnipeg Falcons and they copped the gold medal with polished ease in three games—beating Czechoslovakia, 15-0; the United States, 2-0, and Sweden 12-1.

But victory, as far as Canadians at home were concerned, had been a foregone conclusion. In the intervening four years, however, the natives grew restless over "big talk" by hockey nations overseas, who stressed that the Falcons hadn't been as mighty as anticipated, and that Canada could expect heavy going in the 1924 Games at Chamonix, France.

The news wires made the most of the needling comments and, with whoop-n'-holler, Canada took the bait. We sent over an eight-player team of topnotch star calibre with the press thundering editorial orders to show those upstart hockey nations a spot of "what for."

And that they did, with the most memorable display of powerhouse hockey ever witnessed in the Olympics. The Granites rode roughshod over the five teams they faced with a total of 110 goals for, three against.

They pulverized the Czechs (with Joser Gruss, future obstetrician of note, in goal), 30-0. They steam-rolled Sweden and Switzerland, 22-0 and 33-0, respectively. In the semi-finals they knocked off England, 19-2. In the finals, they took the Americans, 6-1.

The Stalwart Eight consisted of Cyril "Sig" Slater, Reg "Hooley" Smith, Harry Watson, Beattie Ramsay, Jack Cameron, Harold McMunn, Albert J. McCaffrey and Dunc Munro. The only trouble they ran into was trying to keep the goaler (Cameron) and the defencemen from freezing to death on the outdoor rink. During the game against the Czechs, Munro told me some years later, he turned around at one stage to say something to Cameron only to find the nets empty. He was over at the side of the rink posing for a good-looking doll with a camera.

Tex Rickard, the famed promoter of Madison Square Garden, announced in New York that he would sign "the entire Canadian team to represent New York in the National Hockey League." However, Tex got lost in the rush. Montreal Maroons signed Munro. Canadiens got Ramsay. Toronto picked up McCaffrey. Ottawa nabbed the prize package of all, Hooley Smith. Harry Watson, who had scored 13 goals against the Czechs and 13 against the Swiss, was hotly sought after—Toronto's Conn Smythe even had Frank Selke (later boss of the Canadiens) get $5,000 in small bills and stack them on Smythe's desk "just to sign a contract" but Watson refused, preferring to remain an amateur.

Before the Canadians left Chamonix, congratulations were received from St. James's Palace in London, with an invitation from the Prince of Wales, now Duke of Windsor, "to drop in on your way home." Which the Canadians did—but they were a sorry looking lot after Paris.

Hooley Smith, long retired after a 17-season, 200-goal sojourn in the N.H.L., chuckled as he told me of the exhibition game in Paris designed to display the artistry of the Olympic champs.

"Between the champagne parties, excursions to the Folies Bergère and other spots of high culture," he says, "we were pooped out and had to devise a stratagem used for the first and only time in international sport. To get rests—since we had only two subs—our forwards took turns at shooting the puck among the champagne drinks at the tables surrounding the low-rail rinkside. It was messy but effective."

As the years passed, the international aspect of hockey became commonplace. But the Canadians have never ceased to be shocked when one of their hockey teams runs into better teams in faraway places.

Certainly, no aggregation from our younger generation ever received such a surprise as did the ship's hockey team of the Canadian light-cruiser, H.M.C.S. *Ontario*, in Tokyo in 1957.

Hardly had the ship docked when the captain was formally invited to bring the ship's team (with Norm Howe, brother of the famed Gordie, in goal) to the Korakuen Ice Palace for a game against an all-star team picked from the universities of Keio, Waseda, Rikkyo and Meiji.

The invitation came from Prince Tsunemori Takeda as President of the Japan National Skating Union. Although the Canadian sailors hadn't had much opportunity to practise ice hockey on the cruiser's decks, they were in shape, and they figured there was little to worry about from the Gentlemen of Japan who averaged only 160 pounds.

They were quite surprised to learn that Japan had entered an ice-hockey team in Olympic competition twenty-one years before at Garmisch-Partenkirchen, Germany. Also that Tokyo boasted ten artificial ice rinks, fourteen college teams and fifteen semi-pro teams. That Osaka, four hours from Tokyo by rail, and the religious city of Kyoto as well as Nikko, were "hot" hockey centres.

The opening ceremonies, featuring lots of courtesy speeches, were an ordeal with the sailors standing on skates from seven o'clock to eight-thirty. When the game finally got underway, they were amused at the spectators who greeted the most thrilling plays with respectful silence lest applause reflect upon the honourable loser. They also got a big kick out of an early episode which saw a Japanese forward, who had been banished to the sin-bin for boarding, bow to the referee and then to his honourable Canadian victim.

But there wasn't much else for the hockey prides-and-joys of the H.M.C.S. *Ontario*—and particularly for goaler Norm, brother of honourable Gordon—to be amused about. There, in the land of the cherry tree and loquat, our sailors got scuttled, 12-3.

24

CHAPTER THREE

In Case Anyone Asks,
It All Began about 2000 B.C.

Johnny "Goose" McCormack was born in Edmonton in 1925. Thirty years later he made a more notable re-entry as player for Edmonton Flyers in the Western Hockey League, with the status of an N.H.L. veteran who had worn the battle garb of Maple Leafs, Canadiens and Black Hawks. Eventually a radio broadcaster asked the inevitable question: Did he find much difference between the prairie type of hockey and the Big Time?

Johnny replied: "Yeah, here the rink doors are trickier." He went on to tell of his first day at practice when he found one of his younger team mates standing on the ice in front of the rink door. The kid asked: "Would you please open the door for me?"

Johnny reached forward and the door opened with a gentle push. "Why didn't you open it yourself?" he asked. The kid replied: "Wet paint."

The face of hockey has undergone many liftings since the game began, but one feature has remained unchanged with each new generation of player. The rookie invariably regards the veteran as a square.

Certainly, there's something to be said in favour of the rookie, and let not the Hockey Hall of Fame at the Canadian National Exhibition tremble in wrath—every hallowed hero hanging therein was a rookie once himself. Take the case of one so-suspended Frank Clancy.

The last nickname anybody would have thought of pinning

on the five-foot-seven, 127-pound, seventeen-year-old rookie in the Ottawa Senators' camp was "King." When Manager Tommy Gorman signed Clancy and informed the press that he would play defence in one of the slambangest eras hockey has ever known, the press snorted back: "Aw, quit kidding, Tommy!"

When, in the first practice, he was knocked cold while trying to bull through the hardrock defence of Buck Boucher and Eddie Gerard, observers opined the boy should never have left his mother.

Yet in the Senators' very last game of that season—on the night of March 31, 1923—the terrific teenager practically single-handed won the Stanley Cup by playing all six positions.

It happened in Vancouver against Edmonton, and the famed Senators were already on the limp when they went west—with a roster of only nine players. But even at that wee Clancy thought he was lucky just to be able to sit out the game on the bench as utility man.

Then the defence star, Eddie Gerard, got a shoulder separation and in went Clancy. When Gerard was taped together and returned, the other defence star, Buck Boucher, asked for a breather, and Gorman told Clancy to move over. In the second period, the immortal Senator centre, Frank Nighbor, was exhausted, and Clancy replaced him. Then he relieved Cy Denneny on left wing and Punch Broadbent on right for rest periods. But the highlight came when goaler Clint Benedict drew a slashing penalty and, in those days, goalers had to serve it. As Benedict skated off he handed his big stick to Clancy: "Here, kid, take care of the store until I get back."

In later years Clancy insisted he wasn't afraid because he didn't know any better. But Senators were leading 1-0 at the time and it was still that way when Benedict returned. And so it ended. The team trudged back into the dressing-room to pick up the Stanley Cup and the $235 each, their share for winning it. In later years, as a Toronto Maple Leaf front-office executive, Clancy sighed to me: "I was a cocky kid then but what shape I must have been in. I remember looking around at all the gasping veterans and found myself wondering what they looked so dog-tired about."

Another rookie comes to mind, Mel Hill, from Glenboro, Manitoba. The New York Rangers had turned him down for size, figuring he could never stand the long schedule much less any punishing playoffs to follow. He drifted into the Boston Bruins' camp, and Rangers looked good in their decision all season—Hill ended fiftieth in N.H.L. scoring. But that's when the Rangers stopped looking good.

Rangers and Bruins worked their way through the semi-finals in that 1939 playoff series, the last before World War II cut into the league's playing strength. And it proved one of the most gruelling final series of all time, going to the full seven games.

The first game was just a half-minute less than two full games. Hill's goal broke up the marathon mêlée for Bruins. The second game also went into overtime. At 8:24, Hill scored the winner. Bruins won the third, but Rangers came to life, taking three in a row to tie the series. The seventh, and last, went to 48 minutes of overtime. Hill's goal won the Stanley Cup. Can you wonder that he swaggered a mite as Manager Lester Patrick and his Rangers joined the press in paying homage to him?

When, at 1:48 a.m. on April 4, 1933, Toronto Leafs eliminated Boston Bruins in the Cup semi-finals after 164 minutes and 47 seconds of play, it was a rookie to the N.H.L. and the smallest player of both teams who netted the Big One —128-pound Ken Doraty, born in Stittsville, Ontario.

The rousing goal, scored on surging speed and stick-handling around Boston's storied defenceman, Eddie Shore, and goalie, Tiny Thompson, so roused the drowsing press box that Ted

"The Moaner" Reeve wended his way back to Melinda Street and up to his littered desk in *The Telegram* to pound poetically:

It was a winter's evening
In nineteen sixty-two
Old Kaspar sat up in his flat
A-sampling of his brew
While Wilhelmine and Peterkin
The hockey match were tuning in.

And when old Foster Hewitt yelled
"He missed the open net,"
And on the air there came a blare
That rocked the eight-tube set,
Young Peterkin said "This must be
The greatest game in history.

"There's forty thousand in the rink
The series now is tied."
Old Kaspar took another hook
And shook his head and sighed,
"My son you should have been with me
At the Boston game in '33."

Ted Reeve meant to be prophetic, but if Old Kaspar had really been sighing in 1962, it would hardly have been about Doraty's goal. More likely it would have been about another rookie who entered the league a decade after Doraty lighted the lamp. This rookie lived a full N.H.L. life and had already faded from the scene in 1962 after scoring a total of 82 goals in Stanley Cup action alone; he had amassed an overall, regular and playoff, total of 1,091 points (626 goals, 465 assists) in 1,111 games. The name: Maurice "Rocket" Richard.

One could fill quite a chunk of book on rookies who came up to out-dazzle the dazzlers of yesterday. It's plain nonsense for so many old-timers to argue that the game hasn't speeded up and improved many hundred per cent from the old days when replacements were few and speed lagged at the end or when players "ragged" the puck in mid-ice to kill off penalties. When play frequently slowed to a crawl on water-covered ice in an era before the new rules, zoning and forward passing were injected to speed everything up.

It would make just as much sense to argue that runners aren't as strong, as skilled, as fast, as they used to be. In England in August, 1962, five runners in the same race, headed by 128-pound Jim Beatty from Los Angeles, broke the so-long unbreakable, four-minute mile. The sixth runner in that race had a time of 4:01.2 which would have beaten the world-record mile time of Sweden's immortal Gunder Hagg as recently as 1945.

A season or so ago, the Sports College, a fact-finding organization in Toronto, sent a battery of researchers into action to find out just how fast the modern game has become. They found that Chicago's Bobby Hull, for instance, hit 28.2 m.p.h. without the puck in bursts from line to line and 26.4 with the puck. His wrist shot registered 108 m.p.h.

Just as new faces have come and eventually gone in the National Hockey League, so have cities. In and out of the picture have been Ottawa, Hamilton, Quebec City, Pittsburgh, Philadelphia and St. Louis. Gone as well are two other Montreal teams, Wanderers and Maroons. Vanished too is the team that pioneered the way into Madison Square Garden, the Americans of whom you'll read more about later.

On November 22, 1917, in Montreal, the National Hockey League was born in setting both ingenious and hilarious. Only two of the six cities currently in the N.H.L. were represented, Montreal by the Canadiens and Toronto by the Arenas (later St. Pats, later Maple Leafs). Montreal had another representative, the now extinct Wanderers. Ottawa was represented by the Senators and Quebec City by the Bull Dogs. Quebec, after being accepted, asked to be excused for a season for financial reasons. (Quebec returned to action in 1919 and vanished permanently in 1920, selling the franchise to Hamilton. The league got underway on December 19: Canadiens at Ottawa, Toronto at Wanderers. By the way, Toronto was the only city with artificial ice.

Actually, the old National Hockey Association could have carried on—the reason it died is that everybody had a mad on against one Eddie Livingstone, holder of a second Toronto franchise. He was an alert, aggressive sort of fellow but a red flag to other executives in the N.H.A.

These others couldn't legally toss Eddie out so they tossed themselves out. They then rose in a body, marched to a salon nearby and slammed the door. This left Eddie and his lawyer in the hallway with a perfectly good franchise but nobody to play with. Meanwhile the others gleefully formed the N.H.L.

From that bizarre beginning, through many tribulations, rose the greatest hockey show the world has ever known, the National Hockey League of today with an international, six-city audience of more than 2,800,000 annually.

Many have been the Glamour Guys—notably one—responsible. In their own way, equally dramatic and certainly as responsible were many Dollar Daredevils whose stories intrigue me. But, as my research extended, I found myself growing increasingly curious about the birth of the game itself.

This book just isn't big enough to deal in detail with the rival claims of Kingston, Halifax and Montreal as birthplaces of hockey. The fact is that no formal, scientific research has ever been conducted. However, some years ago the Canadian Amateur Hockey Association stated "the best claim" had been made by Kingston, Ontario. Evidence was presented to the effect that members of Her Majesty's Royal Canadian Rifles, an Imperial Army Unit, had played ice hockey to the rear of Tete du Pont barracks in 1855.

But was it hockey? It would seem that the English troops,

lovers of field hockey, wanted to continue playing in winter. Thus the skates and the frozen surface of Kingston Bay. Any number of people could play and ofttimes the goals were one-quarter of a mile apart. Other times goals were nearer due to difficulty in clearing the snow. They continued playing with the field hockey stick and ball.

All this impressed me as being nothing more than makeshift fun and of no historical significance—until one Sunday afternoon in 1963 when I was on assignment for *Weekend Magazine* in Stockholm, Sweden.

Rudy Eklow, sports editor of the *Dagens Nyheter* asked if I'd ever seen a game of bandy? I said no and soon found myself gazing on a stretch of natural ice about the size of a Canadian football field. The teams were eleven on each side. The sticks appeared almost identical with field hockey sticks. They played with a ball the size of a tennis ball, red in colour and made of light, corky material. Aside from skating widely— in big arcs rather than sharp turns—bandy looked much the same as an ice hockey game, in passing, in shooting, in general techniques. I found myself wondering: was it really bandy they used to play on frozen Kingston Bay and not makeshift field hockey?

President Clarence Campbell of the N.H.L. brings his legalistic reasoning into action on the subject whenever it comes up. He insists that ice hockey is so different from any other games bearing a hockey tag that ice hockey has to be regarded as a game unto itself. He asserts: "The game of ice hockey did not exist until the first rules were drawn up and a game was played. As such, ice hockey has to be regarded as strictly Canadian."

A McGill student, J. G. A. Creighton, is credited with being author of the rules under which the first game of "true" ice hockey was played in Montreal in 1875 between two teams drawn from the McGill student body. It would be convenient to wrap up the subject at this point, but it has to be admitted that some confusion has been aroused by further evidence that Creighton had merely "imported" the game as he had seen it played in his native Halifax.

There is also one other spot of confusion. President Campbell admits that he himself was astonished to learn from the late Jock Harty—after whom an arena is named in Kingston—that in the historic first international ice-hockey game, played between McGill and Harvard, a ball was used.

If this is so, when did the puck enter hockey? Until the puck appeared, ice hockey could not have taken on an appearance entirely distinctive from bandy.

The only plausible answer seems to be that, at some point, some ingenious unknown decided to slice a hard ball into a round, flat-surfaced object to see how a sliding rather than a rolling object would behave.

In 1885, Queen's University and the Royal Military College played Canada's first organized hockey game, and "the original puck" is today on display in Queen's Gymnasium. It is a sawed-up lacrosse ball and looks homemade. Yet the official puck of the N.H.L. (the Art Ross Puck), for all its vulcanized rubber material and standardized diameter of three inches, as well as its one-inch thickness, retains a touch of informality —pucks even at major-league level may vary as much as half an ounce in weight (between five and one-half and six ounces).

All of this fits in with the name, puck. Just how it came to be called that, or by whom, nobody knows. But it was aptly named—Webster defines "puck" as "a mischievous sprite or elf."

And whoever did the first slicing job should be in hockey's Hall of Fame because of his contribution to the growth of the game. This was impressed upon me in Sweden. The reason why ice hockey is pushing bandy out of the picture lies in the inability of fans to follow the ball in bandy. A player slams it, golf-like, while on the move, the goaler makes a frantic motion, and the goal judge (standing alongside the huge net) raises his red flag. But nobody has seen the ball (even painted red) whooshing in.

Without seeing the scoring, a game just isn't fun for fans. And one has to conclude that ice hockey, without the puck, would hardly have lived. Certainly it would never have won the rapt attention of so many millions of pairs of eyes whose owners pay such fancy prices to watch the game today.

Yet with every birth there have to be parents. Just as every bouncing baby looks like one of its parents, so does ice hockey. I see our game's fatherhood in bandy and grandfatherhood in field hockey.

If you want to go back any farther, you're welcome, gentle reader. It has been found recorded on stone tablets in Persia that field hockey was played there in 2000 B.C. But don't ask me for the lineups—the Persian sports writer must have pooped out pounding.

CHAPTER FOUR

When $850 Paid Hockey a Multi-Million Dividend

At the climax of Walter "Babe" Pratt's hectic twelve-year career in the N.H.L. with Rangers, Maple Leafs and Bruins, during which he won the Hart (most valuable player) Trophy award once and all-star recognition twice, he was waived out of the League.

Bruins announced they were shipping the ex-star down to Hershey in the American Hockey League. A reporter asked Babe what he thought about it?

"I think," said Babe, "I'd better start saving my money."

Money has been called "filthy lucre," "root of all evil" and "lovely green stuff." Take your pick, but the fact is that either Pratt or the N.H.L. would have had considerable difficulty remaining alive without it.

Happily, however, money happens to be the least of the N.H.L.'s worries today. More than $7,500,000 pours into the six-rink coffers annually through the box offices and probably another $10,000,000 through the concessions.

Yet history indicates that this golden flood might have been a mere trickle if it hadn't been for the $850 in small-denomination bills heaped on a table in the parlour of a home in Stratford, Ontario, on July 7, 1923. The green heap proved the deciding argument in getting an intermediate player, named Howie Morenz, to sign a Montreal Canadiens contract. It provided $2,500 covering the 1923/24 schedule of twenty-four games.

The backstage story on the signing ranges from ribald to

rollicking, but subsequent events proved it to be a moment momentous in the history of hockey. The electric excitement sparked by Morenz did more than any other single factor to establish the National Hockey League in the United States.

He skated into immediate stardom. Within a few seasons the New York Rangers were to offer $60,000 for him, and the Montreal Maroons promptly raised it to $75,000—a figure comparable to $200,000 today. Canadiens refused with: "Morenz is beyond price."

From his first game in Toronto, when he scored all the Canadiens' goals, the breath-taking rookie spearheaded the team all the way to the Stanley Cup, in turn roaring through three great title teams, Ottawa, Vancouver and Calgary. He was top scorer in the playoffs.

In his sophomore season, when Boston Bruins of 1924/25 became the first American entry in the N.H.L., Morenz zoomed into super-stardom. By 1926, he was being tagged by American scribes as "the Babe Ruth of hockey."

Other factors contributed to the big rush of 1926/27 which saw not one but six American teams in the league. As the Bambino, whose slugging captivated the public imagination and projected baseball from a restricted sports field into general entertainment, so did the spectacular scoring and glittering gambles of young Morenz captivate tens of thousands of Americans who had never before even seen a hockey game. He was a headline living up to exalted status on the sports pages; overnight he converted curious customers into fervent fans.

True, hockey had made some inroads into the United States before Morenz, but none had led to the Big Time.

The same year, 1893, that Lord Stanley of Preston, then Governor-General of Canada, donated a cup worth $48.66 to hockeydom, two Yale tennis stars, Malcolm G. Chace and Arthur E. Foote, returned from tournaments in Canada with such glowing reports of a game called ice hockey that it was "tried out" at New Haven University in Connecticut. Almost simultaneously, C. Shearer, a Montrealer studying at Johns Hopkins University in Baltimore, whipped up enough interest to promote a team that took on a visiting Quebec team in an exhibition which caught collegian fancy there.

The game spread quickly. Three years later the first league was formed in the United States, the four-team Amateur Hockey League. Two months later saw a league formed in Baltimore. By the end of the 1896/97 winter, there were teams playing throughout New England, in Philadelphia, Pittsburgh, Chicago and Washington, D.C.

Pro hockey came in dramatic fashion with the Canadians playing under the American flag in the small Michigan mining town of Houghton in 1903. The Portage Lakers won twenty-four of twenty-six games but couldn't win lasting favour with fandom.

The Pacific Coast League of Canada admitted a member from the United States (Portland) in 1914, and a year later Seattle also entered. In 1917 the Seattle Metropolitans, "loaded" with star Canadian imports, beat Montreal Canadiens to send the Stanley Cup south of the border for the first time.

When, in 1925, major hockey disbanded in the west, there were three American cities entered in the N.H.L. for 1925/26. To the Boston Bruins, now a year old, had been added the Pittsburgh Pirates and the New York Americans.

The entry of New York was the key needed to open the door to an opulent future for the N.H.L.—if the game would click there—because then as now Manhattan was the pulse of what sport regards as Big Time. Other American cities may come up with better teams and greater stars, but, without New York's approving participation, no sport seems to achieve the summit in national fan acceptance.

When Boston provided an American debut for the N.H.L. in 1924, George H. "Tex" Rickard was ruling the old Madison Square Garden where Harry Thaw had shot Stanford White.

At the time Tex was mulling over final plans for the new Madison Square Garden, but the blueprints didn't include an ice plant. To be frank, nobody in all the forty-eight states was less interested in "that Canadian game" than Tex. But he was irked enough with Boston's favourable reaction to listen poker-faced to one Tom Duggan who had bought a franchise from the N.H.L. and sold it to Boston.

The role of Tom Duggan was an odd one but a tremendous contribution nonetheless to the expansion of hockey into the United States. A Montrealer (his son, Frank, is an artist with the *Montreal Star*), Tom owned two racetracks there, Mount Royal and King's Park. He also owned a "piece" of Coney Island in New York and was in with one Bill Dwyer on a racetrack at Cincinnati.

Tom was a promoter at heart and he thought hockey a "natural" for the United States. He went to the N.H.L. and asked to purchase three brand-new franchises for $7,000 apiece. The N.H.L. was only too glad to pick up $21,000 out of the blue and handed over the three sets of papers.

One was sold to Boston and another to Pittsburgh. Then he made Tex Rickard his No. 1 target. It was a rough go with more ups and downs than the British had in the Common Market huddles. Duggan used to wander back, dejected and despairing, to the A. & E. Club in New York, where he'd sit with a group of other Canadian-borns awaiting the latest news. The moans would eventually turn into roars against Rickard. On one occasion an ex-Canadian sports editor, Bill MacBeth, then writing racing for the *New York Tribune*, had to be restrained from leaving to "sock Tex in the nose."

Eventually Duggan approached Tex with an invitation to visit Montreal to "have a look at the Canadiens and Morenz,"

Tex agreed, one suspects, for two reasons: to get Duggan out of his thinning hair, and to get away from prohibition in the United States for an interlude in the gushing oasis of Montreal.

It took only one game. Tex was bitten by the hockey bug and rushed back (smuggling a platinum hangover through customs) to New York in time to alter the Madison Square plans. In went an ice plant. Tex was also shrewd enough to insist on getting an established team of N.H.L. calibre to go along with the ice plant. What's more, he told Duggan he didn't want to pay for it.

Duggan, the hockey salesman extraordinary, promptly turned to the Hamilton Tigers. They had finished atop the league in 1924/25 only to default to the Canadiens when the players actually went on strike for a better slice of the playoff melon. The fans and press were so "down" on the Tigers that an offer to buy was listened to with more than passing interest. They came up with a price of $75,000—not a bad profit on the $5,000 spent only five years before to purchase the franchise from Quebec City.

Duggan then talked his racing partner, big Bill Dwyer, into buying the Tigers and taking them into New York as the Americans. At that time Bill was well known by everybody in Manhattan who was anybody. In fact, he was the city's top bootlegger and, as investigation later proved, he controlled the entire liquor supply entering prohibition-ridden New York. He catered to government bosses at state and municipal level as well as blue-bloods and police chiefs. The same investigation later proved that his frequent rush deliveries were made to bigwigs by the fire department!

While writing this book I asked Frank Duggan if his late Dad hadn't felt any uneasiness over escorting bottlegger Dwyer into major hockey as an owner?

"Not a bit," replied Frank, "for the simple reason that in New York in that period of prohibition the bootlegger wasn't yet the obnoxious personality now seen being shot on TV by Elliott Ness. He was a very popular guy—the friend in need when a good case of Scotch was needed to fortify captains of industry around the conference table or in more gladsome surroundings. Instead of a personage operating outside the law, he was more of a genial St. Bernard plodding daringly and dauntlessly through the snow with brandy barrel on neck to humans in distress. What's more, Dwyer was possibly an ideal choice as a peddler of tickets for the introduction of major hockey—those who didn't buy might have had their booze cut off."

Frank Duggan was a guest of his father's when Tex Rickard and party were brought up for the look-see at hockey in Montreal. Frank recalls sitting with the late Damon Runyon, then New York's top sports writer—on everything except hockey.

"Runyon, a silent type, watched the activity without comment for two periods," said Frank, "before leaning over to me and commenting: 'I don't know whether or not you've noticed it, but that guy with the pads is shoving the puck out everytime somebody tries to push it in.' "

At that time in Montreal, the late George Lawrence was a readers' favourite on hockey while doubling in brass as sports writer and sports cartoonist with the *Montreal Herald*. Frank tells of Rickard cornering Lawrence with an offer: "Name your own price and come to New York—we need a fellow like you badly down there."

Lawrence shook his head. "Sorry, Tex, but I wouldn't think of moving to any country that has prohibition."

Tex Rickard now had a rink, an ice plant and an established team for which he hadn't paid a cent. He now turned on his promotional flare—the same flare that made history in the form of the first world championship heavyweight boxing extravaganzas. Tex's first move was to work pressure on Frank

Calder, then the N.H.L. president, to line up the 1925/26 schedule so that the opening game in Madison Square would present as opposition "those Flying Frenchmen from Montreal with Morenz." Calder, exalting in the entry of New York, was only too happy to co-operate. So it was the Canadiens versus the Americans, December 15, 1925.

Tex must have known he was inviting a shellacking—Canadiens won, 3-1—but he had concentrated on glamour, glamour on the ice as well as in the stands. He had wooed a black-tie society crowd by an old dodge. By donating a percentage of the proceeds to charity, he had the social *élite* of New York working as ticket salesmen for the game.

Because society was "behind" the opener, the band of the Governor-General's Footguards, adorned smartly in scarlet, made the trip from Ottawa. On hearing the Footguards were coming, Tex had no trouble in selling the West Point Cadets' band on attending, adorned in blue uniforms that fitted like wallpaper.

Jimmy Walker, shortly to become "Mr. New York" as its best-dressed and most careless mayor ever, was bouncing and beaming around the box-seat area. The Prince of Wales had donated a trophy for the occasion. It was strictly Big Time. Not only did the O.K. Stamp by New York arouse other American cities' urgent interest, but it also stamped "finis" on the western league. Players and Stanley Cup moved east, for keeps.

The next season saw the N.H.L. teams boosted to ten—it was the biggest single year in N.H.L. history. Besides Ottawa, Toronto, Montreal's two teams (Canadiens and Maroons), the Americans, Pittsburgh and Boston, there were now Chicago's Black Hawks, Detroit's Cougars (later Red Wings) and a second New York team, the Rangers. That season not only saw Morenz come up with a 25-goal effort (in a 44-game schedule) but also personally convert the most respected and

40

influential sports writer of the New York era, the *New York Time's* John Kieran, into a rabid fan. It was Kieran who startled American sport fans to their innards with a poem entitled: "I'll Take Hockey Every Time." It read in part:

I'm a fairly peaceful man, and an old-time baseball fan,
You can hear me yell when Heilmann hits the ball;
And I howl when Ty Cobb stabs one, and I growl when
    Speaker grabs one.
And I roar when Babe Ruth's homer clears the wall.
But the diamond sport is quiet to that reeling, rousing
    riot,
To a slashing game of hockey in its prime;
It's a shindig wild and gay; it's a battle served frappé;
Give me hockey—I'll take hockey—any time!

I've an ever-ready ear for a rousing football cheer,
And I love to see a halfback tackled low,
It's a really gorgeous sight when the boys begin to fight
With a touchdown only half a yard to go.
But take all the most exciting parts of football, baseball,
    fighting,
And then mix them up to make a game sublime,
Serve it up with lots of ice, you don't have to ask me
    twice,
Give me hockey—I'll take hockey—any time!

Over Chicago way, Major Frederic McLaughlin, heading a sports-minded group of citizens and armed with $250,000, had bought the Portland team from the defunct western circuit and added a few other top players. He and his wife, the glamorous stage personality Irene Castle, beamed as the new-born Chicago Black Hawks made a spectacular debut by beating Toronto, 4-1, at the old Coliseum. Of the 7,600 fans present, it was estimated that ninety-five per cent had never seen Canada's national game before.

I looked up the old press files on a recent visit to Chicago. The *Daily Tribune* reported: "The press men were absolutely flabbergasted by their first glimpse of hockey at the Coliseum." But the *Herald* and *Examiner* matched in prose Kieran's poesy: "The fastest game Chicago has seen since the ember-laden winds of '71 raced with the fire department was witnessed last night at the Coliseum. Pro ice hockey is faster than horse racing, dog racing and pugilistic punch telegraphy. Lightning itself with an Ederle coat of grease has to be stepped up to compete with Eskimo Polo as demonstrated last evening."

The writer did, however, look upon the art of goalkeeping with jaundiced eye: "The goaler has the laziest job next to foreman of an ice-cutting gang on the Panama Canal. He's padded worse than some political payrolls. All he has to do is spread himself and he can stop the puck—but it is a contest between puck and luck."

This was a vital "missionary period" for the N.H.L. in the United States. The initial impact had to be both impressive and lasting. It was a foregone conclusion that the cynical and restless American fan wouldn't keep coming just to sit and study the sciences of a strange game.

Baseball, I have always figured, requires two years to "sell" a mystified onlooker into becoming a fan. But just as one didn't need to be a knowledgeable fan to appreciate the thunder of Babe Ruth's bat, neither did one need to "know" hockey to be lifted by the thrills of Morenz.

I remember him then as he zoomed into his peak with only two speeds, fast and faster. In that last season (1926/27), before the introduction of the forward pass, the defencemen usually refrained from much rushing and would be found lined up, side by side, in front of the net. Most forwards tried to get around them; Morenz just as often tried to hurtle through them.

Time and time again he'd go down with bone-rattling body-checks, often he'd get caught squarely in the "sandwich." But he'd come back and leave the crowd aghast as he'd hurtle through, pick up the puck and score—or nearly score. On several occasions I saw this meteoric Morenz bowl over both defencemen with sheer, reckless savagery.

Like the Babe who used to pack a thrill even striking out, Morenz in missing was an experience. He also served another notable purpose, educating fans.

Babe Ruth's colossal clouts captivated the new fan but, simultaneously, his offensive might draw fans' attention to other appealing aspects of the game. The outfielder whose daring dash to make a backhanded, one-handed catch of what seemed a sure, inside-the-park homer or the shortstop who made a lofty, leaping catch of a sizzling liner were now appreciated. The home-team pitcher who held the Bambino hitless was appreciated outside New York; when a visiting pitcher hand-cuffed the Babe in Yankee Stadium, it built up to a duel that often climaxed with a soul-satisfying four-bagger on their next meeting.

So it was in hockey with Morenz.

In that 1926/27 season, there was a newcomer in the league from Fort Qu'Appelle, Saskatchewan. His name was Eddie Shore, a hardrock defenceman who put growl into the Boston Bruins and created a massive impact on the rookie American fan. His sheer sockeroo in bodychecking plus direct-line counter-rushing carried the message to rookie fans that there was such a thing as defensive skill, too. But I really think he needed comparison with such as Morenz, the strictly offensive head-liner, to be fully appreciated by the rookie fan.

There were plenty of other great hockey players in the league that season: Toronto's Happy Day and Ace Bailey; Maroon's dazzling Nels Stewart, who had led the league in scoring the previous season as a rookie; Rangers' Cook brothers and Frank Boucher; Chicago's Dick Irvin (later destined for further fame as a coach) and Babe Dye; Americans' Billy Burch and Lionel Conacher; Ottawa's Cy Denneny and King Clancy; Detroit's Frank Frederickson and Duke Keats; Pittsburgh's Baldy Cotton and Hib Milks. But, as in the case of Shore, their less-dramatic skills were appreciated only when pitted against dramatic opposition as personified by Morenz.

The art of playmaking, for example, was impressed on the American writer through Morenz. It took a while for them to appreciate just what a 133-pound line mate like Aurel Joliat was contributing in the care of feeding headliner Morenz. Joliat aided and abetted the entire Morenz career with the Canadiens from left wing.

Normally, Morenz as a centre should have been the play-maker, but coaches of that era weren't sticklers for positional hockey—as long as the goals came the coaches didn't care how they came. Morenz loved lots of ice, not a lane down which to roam, and wee Aurel had a sixth sense about where the human missile was likely to be in the next second or so.

In 1962, I met up with Joliat in Ottawa where at age sixty, he was working in an information wicket at the Union Station. He described what he rated "the goal of goals" scored by Morenz and the vivid description remains in my mind like a movie.

It was the goal that won the Stanley Cup for the Canadiens in 1931. The semi-finals had been a gruelling grind; Boston had extended the five-game series to the limit, with three of the games ending in overtime. Now, in the finals against Chicago, it was a continuation of the grind. Two of the best-of-five series' games had gone into overtime and now they were in No. 5. From somewhere down deep, Morenz found the blazing desire for an explosive effort. Joliat now takes over:

> Morenz had rushed away from us with the puck down centre and was checked at the Chicago defence. Some Chicago forward picked up the loose puck at the gallop and I checked him at mid-ice. I had taken only two strides when I heard "Joliat!" screamed at me from right wing.

Even with play going at top speed Morenz had raced back on my left wing, whirled around behind me and had again picked up a full head of steam down right wing. To catch him before he hit the blue line I had to fire a shot at him rather than a pass. Howie picked up the puck as if he were using a lacrosse stick and without losing stride. He was through the defence, in on goalie Chuck Gardiner and rifling the puck into a corner before any of us fully knew what was happening.

It seems incredible that Canadiens had left this Morenz dangling for ten months unsigned in Stratford, while the Toronto St. Pats remained only casually interested in this gold mine in their back yard.

Leo Dandurand, boss man of the Canadiens in 1923, first heard of Morenz from an old player, Ernie Sauve, who had refereed a game between two C.N.R. motive-power teams, Stratford and Montreal. He told Dandurand that "a kid named Morenz scored so many goals they had to yank him."

A month later while in Toronto, Dandurand asked Lou Marsh, then refereeing as well as writing sports for the *Toronto Star*, to have a look at the kid on his next trip to Stratford. More time passed, then a rave report from Marsh. Dandurand sent Riley Hearn, old-time Wanderer goalie, to Stratford with an offer of a $2,500 contract. Young Howie rejected the offer, and Dandurand shrugged the matter off as he left to attend to racing interests extending as far as Salt Lake City. In July, Marsh caught up with Dandurand on long distance.

"Better hurry," said Marsh, "St. Pats are warming up. Use cash, the kid has some small debts around town."

Dandurand promptly sent Cecil Hart (later his successor as the Canadiens' pilot) to Stratford with the stack of bills worth $850, and Hart piled them on the table. Howie gasped and

45

signed. Because he was only twenty-years old, the father signed, too.

A storm of astounding dimension blew up. In Toronto, Dandurand was accused of "legalized kidnapping." Stratford fans heaped abuse on the flabbergasted Howie for deserting Ontario to play in Quebec. A minister began a letter-to-the-editor campaign blasting the Canadiens for taking an under-age boy away from his home-life for the "wicked wiles of Montreal."

On August 10, Howie wrote a letter which Dandurand showed me. Its attractive handwriting immediately catches the eye, reminding one of the lost art in modern schools. Attached was the signed contract and a certified cheque for $850. The letter read:

> Dear Sir:
> I am enclosing check and contract to play with your club owing to several reasons of which family and work are the most to consider. I find it impossible to leave Stratford. I am sorry if I have caused you expense and inconvenience and trust you will accept the returned contract in a sportsmanlike way.
>
> Yours very truly,
>
> HOWARD MORENZ

Dandurand could only see plotting by the Toronto St. Pats behind the letter. He blew a fuse and told the press: "If Morenz doesn't play in Montreal, he'll play pro hockey nowhere."

A sympathetic friend tipped off Dandurand that young Howie was getting $800 a season in Stratford. Dandurand promptly informed the Ontario Hockey Association executive: "I'll blow the lid off amateur hockey if you don't persuade Morenz to observe his contract."

Then Howie Morenz went to Montreal asking to be released.

While explaining how unhappy everybody was, he actually broke down and cried. Dandurand, the personification of French-Canadian polish and courtesy, dropped the "hard" pro sport approach. He told the weeping Howie to forget about everything until after lunch.

From another phone he sent an S.O.S. to all available Canadiens' players to rush by taxis to luncheon in an exclusive down-town restaurant. Howie, naturally well-versed in the N.H.L. rosters, went popeyed as he entered, was introduced and seated between the famed Cleghorn brothers, Sprague and Odie.

An afternoon and dinner in the gracious setting of Dandurand's opulent home occupied the rest of the day to train time. At the station, Dandurand told Howie to report to training camp at Grimsby, Ontario, and, if he wasn't happy after two weeks, "we'll have another talk."

Howie reported but the pressure was intense. An average of ten long-distance calls per day came from Stratford fans. He was so unhappy by Saturday that he asked to go home for the weekend.

"We had a Sunday practice slated," recalled Dandurand, "and I didn't dare leave camp because my hardened veterans would carve the rookies to pieces. So I rented a car and had a druggist named Farrell take Howie home with orders to get him back Monday, bound and gagged if necessary. He came back—unhappier than ever."

And he stayed unhappy right up to the opening game at Toronto with most of Stratford's populace making the trip to cheer him. Canadiens lost, 7-2, but the kid scored both Canadiens' goals. From that night on, Howie never looked back.

Within a few weeks he had attained the star status it had taken others years to reach. In 1929/30, he hit his peak and helped thousands of crash-shocked fans on both sides of the border to forget their financial troubles by blasting forty goals and assisting on ten others in a forty-four game schedule.

Eleven seasons after joining the Canadiens, the blistering pace began to show on the thirty-two year old, one hundred and sixty-five pound Morenz. Montreal's harsh fandom, apparently mistaking fading legs for fading desire, began booing their former idol. Raging mad, Leo Dandurand made a stern decision. To save Howie the humiliation of further experiences in the rink he had grown to regard as home, Dandurand sold him to Chicago for 1934/35.

Howie came up with eight goals and assisted on twenty-six others as Coach Clem Loughlin had him concentrate on play-making instead of his familiar trigger-man role. But Howie's heart wasn't in Chicago, his relationship with management went sour and part way through 1935/36, he was traded to the Rangers for Glenn Brydson.

In New York, he got a royal welcome. John Kieran, the *Times*' now dyed-in-the-wool hockey fan, exalted with a column on January 28th, 1936, which was headed: "Here Comes Howie!"

Kieran went into the colour and speed of the Swift Swiss he had known in other days and reminded his readers that tonight would see the high-goal quartet of the current N.H.L. on Garden ice in the same game: Howie Morenz, Bill Cook, Aurel Joliat and Frank Boucher. Wrote Kieran: "For ten years or more these are the marksmen who have led in the raining of rubber into the nets."

The part-season with Rangers was a happy one, but in the summer of 1936 a dramatic move brought him back to the Canadiens. Cecil Hart, who had been replaced as coach by Newsy Lalonde, returned to the pilot post. One of his conditions on accepting was that the club bring back Howie "to play out the rest of his N.H.L. career with his own Canadiens." Which is exactly what Howie did.

The fickle fans, mayhap feeling remorse, gave Howie the

welcome of a returning hero, and he responded at age thirty-four with a monumental comeback attempt. On the night of January 28, 1937, he hurtled into the Chicago defence in a game at the Forum with all the reckless abandon of his youth. Defenceman Earl Seibert got a piece of Howie who went crashing sideways into the boards at the St. Catherine Street end of the rink. A leg snapped.

Complications developed and, on March 8th, 1937, the mighty heart stopped. The body lay in state at mid-ice in the Forum with hockey's top stars alternating as guard of honour day and night. His funeral service, held on the exact spot where he had been in thousands of faceoffs, saw Howie pack the Forum for the last time. Another 200,000 lined the streets in sub-zero weather as the cortege passed en route to Mount Royal Cemetery.

It was while attending the Forum service, Leo Dandurand told me years later, that it really dawned on him how significant in hockey history had been the hectic period involving the signing of young Howie fourteen years before.

If St. Pats had signed him, the team, shy on glamour, would have soared into the sun instead of going on the selling block. If Maroons' bid for him had been accepted, the team would certainly have weathered the grim depression years and not folded up. If Canadiens had missed Morenz, would they have been able to survive any more than Maroons to become hockey's oldest and most prosperous major club today?

If Howie, serene in his beloved Stratford, hadn't turned pro, how much would all hockey have suffered without the pulsating appeal of the 467 goals he either scored (270), or assisted in scoring, in some 500 games? How many fans south of the border would have remained bogged in indifference without this hockey version of Babe Ruth?

Dandurand shivered. It wasn't because the Forum was chilly; the very presence of Morenz, dead or alive, warmed a rink.

49

CHAPTER FIVE

Brawn over Brain:
If It Works, Why Not?

Incongruously, Lionel Conacher, M.P., best all-round athlete Canada ever produced, died in a softball game against the Press on Parliament Hill. Stories told about him are legion. My favourite was from the days he led the madcap 1933/34 Chicago team to the Stanley Cup. Among the hottest fans was Tony Canzoneri, then between reigns as lightweight champion of the boxing world.

Conacher asked him who was the greatest fighter he had ever met?

"Kid Chocolate," replied Canzoneri. "He was hard to hit because he had a tiny little head and a tiny little waist."

"Well, how did you beat him?" asked Conacher.

Said Canzoneri: "By hitting him in his tiny little head and his tiny little waist."

Critics of N.H.L.-style hockey claim it's projecting into multi-million homes through television an incessant triumph of brawn over brain. One longhair has classed it as a reversal to the "frontal attack" psychology, out-moded since the Charge of the Light Brigade and World War I head-on assaults into mouths of guns became identified as silly slaughter adorned with the veneer of undeniable courage. These critics advocate more stress on strategy, for the foe, diverting and slipping around his flank—or somethin'.

But suppose the opposition is a superior hockey team physically? And mentally superior as well—who just won't be outfoxed? What now, gentle critic? Would you simply admit defeat and revert to the sporting solace of "It's not who wins but how you play the game"?

That sort of thinking ignores a fundamental of the game called hockey. The use of brawn is strictly legal and, make no mistake about it, many a superior team is whittled down to equality by physical contact applied when and where most effective.

Just as Canzoneri, facing a skilled boxer offering minimum target, waded into and through the opposition's defence to conquer, so did the Morenz, Nels Stewart and Rocket Richard of our yesteryears, so do the Gordie Howe, Bobby Hull and Boom Boom Geoffrion of the modern era. If the "brain" approach doesn't work, super-stars forget science and wade in to blast—if the puck doesn't go in, blast at anything that looks like a rebound. Ofttimes I've seen these surging stars end in the net with the goaler—and just as often the puck is in there with them.

The Rocket often reminded interviewers that "those goal-keepers are pretty good too." He told me of countless rushes in on such as Frank Brimsek, Terry Sawchuk and Glenn Hall when "my plan didn't work because they out-smarted me." On such nights, he ruefully confessed, "I often made my mind a blank on going in, figuring that if I didn't know what I was going to do neither could the goaler."

This appears to be rich endorsation of the emphasis on brawn over brain criticism. But what's overlooked is that many a split-second move made by the Rocket without apparent plan was the result of extraordinary skills built through long hours of practice, zealous regard for conditioning, immense physical stamina and lightning reflexes.

The greatest goal ever scored in hockey history—a sweeping statement but nobody has ever dared question it—was the one Rocket scored on April 8, 1952, to knock the Boston Bruins out of the playoff semi-finals. He had been carried off, unconscious and deeply gashed on the forehead after a brutal tumble amid skates, knees and sticks at the Bruin defence. When he returned to the bench in the last period the score was 1-1. Line mate Elmer Lach told me the Rocket sat staring at the clock, his eyes "seemed unable to focus." Yet he insisted on skating out at the next change. That was the memorable time he picked up the puck at his own end and actually carried it end-to-end, through the entire Boston team, button-hooking around one star defenceman (Bill Quackenbush) and bulling by another (Bob Armstrong) to blast the netting behind the lunging goalie (Sugar Jim Henry) with his last ounce of strength.

Rocket sure didn't "think" his way to that Big One for the simple reason that he couldn't. He admitted he learned how it happened only from the morning papers. But this admission skimmed over the fact that his automatic reactions to changing situations had been the result of building his human hockey machine for supreme efforts against the sternest checking. What's often classed as "a lucky goal" was scored many practices before.

Among the Brawn-over-Brain critics there are many who, I honestly believe, are sincere in their belittling of the modern game, but it is largely prompted by their failure to see, or appreciate, what happens out on the ice today. And I don't wonder—the biggest moments are often blurs of action.

Maybe, as the critics charge, hockey has lost a lot since the passing of Kitty-bar-the-door tactics, first developed by Ottawa Senators who could erect a defensive wall to protect a one-goal lead for a whole period. But hockey also gained a lot, as the turnstiles testify, by putting accent on the positive. As a boy in the Montreal Forum, I sold programmes to crowds of 900; today finds the same structure in its dozenth year of sell-outs, with an application list for season tickets five thousand names long. As I write, the N.H.L. rinks have been averaging one

In style, speed and shot, Canadiens' immortal Howie Morenz (left)
lives again today in Chicago's great Bobby Hull (right).

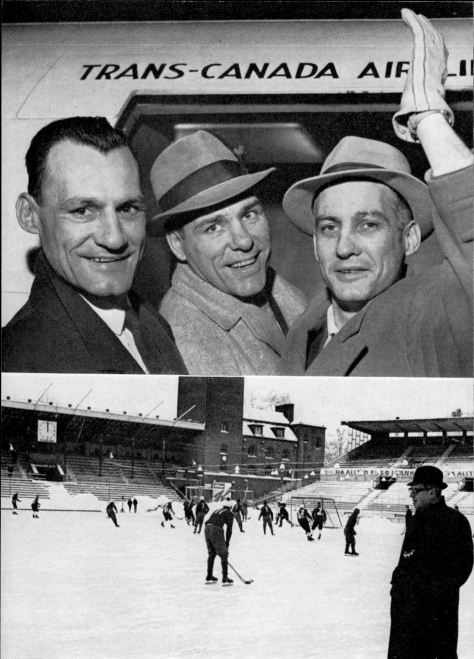

The rollicking, raw-meat Warwick brothers who led the Penticton V's to World Cup in 1955: left to right are Grant, Bill and Dickie.

In Stockholm, Sweden, the author watches a game of bandy. It is field hockey on ice and the author sees this game as "the father of ice hockey."

thousand more customers a game than at the same time in 1961/62 which was a record season.

"Fire-wagon hockey," so vividly introduced by the Canadiens of the Morenz period, is based on one fundamental principle— "get the puck up to the team mate ahead of you." It matters not if the other team scores four as long as you score five. Don't waste time trying to "think" your way down the ice, get it up . . . . up . . . up and skip the fancy shooting; blaze away at the net and not at an opening which won't be there anyway if you take time to look, aim and fire!

Despite the immense increase in goalkeeping skills, fire-wagon hockey has resulted in what produces the cheers and packs the pews—namely goals, more goals. In 1961/62 there were 1,264 goals scored in two hundred and ten N.H.L. games, as compared with 1,090 in the same number of games only ten seasons before.

The evolution to all-out offensive hockey has been gradual. I suppose one has to trace it back to an apparently innocuous rule change in 1920/21 which permitted goalers to pass the puck forward in defensive areas. Prior to the change they used to steer a stopped puck to the side for a mate to collect. Now a swift counter-offensive could begin from a goaler's pass-up.

In 1927-28, forward passes were allowed in defending and centre zones, while goalers' pads were trimmed from twelve inches across to ten. In 1928/29, forward passing was allowed in all three zones, but a pass had to end within the same zone in which it started.

Then came the "red line" across mid-ice.

The change, in 1943/44, permitted a player in the defending zone to pass the puck up to a mate anywhere on his side of centre ice.

The great Boston Bruins team of the preceding years were mainly responsible for the change and, if you must name one player more than any other, it was Eddie Shore. He would bull his way with the puck up to and just over the defending blue line and dump it into a corner. The Kraut Line (Milt Schmidt, Bobby Bauer and Woody Dumart) would follow to hem the puck in. There was also Ray Getliffe, the harshest body-checker in forechecking I have ever seen. A frantic defender would barely get his stick on the puck and start to wheel when caught by a bone-rattling Getliffe bodycheck. Ray relished rock-'n'-roll.

Incidentally, in this lies the key difference between N.H.L. and International Ice Hockey Federation rules which restrict bodychecking to one's own half of the ice. It is claimed, and I concur, that too many injuries result from forechecking body-checks when the receiver isn't "set."

The red-line rule forced the attackers to hold back. At least the attacking defenceman could no longer venture as per-sistently over the defending blue line lest a pass be picked up behind him with nothing but clear ice all the way to his own goal.

Other changes aiming at more speed entered. It was ruled that ice surfaces had to be re-flooded between periods to pre-vent "slow-ice" from developing. Whereas changes in playing personnel used to wait for a stoppage of play, permission was granted to make changes on the fly.

This, by the way, has developed into a skill all its own and well worth while studying. Coaches tell me on-the-fly changing in a speed-crazy game often happens so fast that they cannot keep track of their own players. Rudy Pilous, while coaching Chicago, pointed out how hard that made it to assign a top checker to concentrate on a player such as Gordie Howe.

"Howe often tumbles over the boards from the Detroit bench across the rink," said Pilous, "leaving my checker on the Chicago bench for two minutes or so, because the play has remained too far away from the Chicago bench to get my man into action. And it is surprising how often the play goes for two or three minutes without a whistle or other stoppage."

The fire-wagon style is also dramatically exemplified by the plays developed by teams in recent seasons against the power play. You now see short-handed teams breaking one man loose for a long pass-out, whereas it used to be that such emergencies were met only for desperate checking and icing of the puck until the penalized player returned. I often think back to the old days when each team had an expert at "ragging the puck." He would simply hold on to it around his own end or centre ice. There was a lot of pretty stick-handling, but action sure slowed down for the extent of short-handedness.

Other moves were made to cut down delays. One notable one has almost eliminated the "second fight" on the penalty bench. It used to be that a player who got the worst of it in a brawl on the ice almost invariably tried to "save face" by an encore brawl in the sin-bin.

Now a second major penalty in the same game automatically adds a Misconduct Penalty (ten minutes added to five) plus a $25 fine. A third major penalty brings a Game Misconduct Penalty (remainder of the game) plus a $50 fine. A player has to be a very peeved lad to stay that way that long.

In the sphere of brawling and blood-letting, there is no doubt that official harshness has diverted energy toward hockey instead of havoc.

Sure, it's still a violent pastime but nothing compared to earlier days of major hockey. In an interview I had with Sprague Cleghorn shortly before his death, he admitted to disabling three players on one night in Ottawa, being arrested for almost killing Newsy Lalonde another night in Toronto (Newsy pleaded for Sprague in court and got him off with a $200 fine) and laying-out Lionel Hitchman, of Ottawa Senators, to precipitate the 1923 riot in Montreal's old Mount Royal Arena. In summarizing, Sprague figured he'd been in fifty "stretcher-case" fights. All of this tended to distract as well as delay.

Until two seasons or so ago, defencemen were specialists in falling atop the puck or gathering it into their body to relieve pressure by forcing a whistle. Now this calls for a minor penalty. Even a goaler is subject to the same penalty if he so acts outside his goal crease.

A pet trick for a tired team was to fake an injury. Now the play continues (unless a serious injury is evident) until the injured player's team gets possession of the puck. Thus a faking fella would only be giving the opposition a man advantage.

What happened to those long discussions at bench-side between coach and players over such issues as getting a new stick? Rule 76 empowers a referee to warn the team captain ("C" on sweater) or alternate captain ("A" on sweater) that his team has fifteen seconds in which to resume play. If that fails, the referee calls a bench penalty (one player selected by manager or coach serves a minor) against the team. If that fails, the manager or coach is fined $100. If that fails the game is forefeited to the non-offending club and the case goes to the president for further action.

The ever-increasing list of added incentive bonuses have paid off in terms of more goals, and more goals demand more speed. In the case of the scoring championship (Art Ross Trophy), for example, it used to be that a few select super-stars would take charge fairly early in the season and stay on top. In 1962/63, it was decided to award $500 to the player leading the scoring ($250 for second) at the end of the first half of the schedule. The same amounts would be given to the top scorers of the second half. Over and above that, the aggregate winner and runner-up receive $1,000 and $500 respectively.

This so stimulated scoring that, at the two-thirds way in the schedule, the top fourteen point-getters were divided by only thirteen points, and Johnny Bucyk of the tail-end Bruins topped all.

This breakdown in added incentive bonuses to half-seasons

was spread to all other trophies as well as to all-star teams. All this "forces" hockey into sustained high-gear action; obviously those in line for bonuses work hard, and it also stirs non-contending mates to extra effort, lest they let down contending mates.

In this hurry-hurry atmosphere, brawn is vital, but it just wouldn't be enough to keep a player up in the N.H.L. for long without liberal blending of brain with brain.

I once asked Rangers' Andy Bathgate what had been the turning point for him to stardom. "When confidence came," he replied. "Twice Rangers brought me up only to send me down to Vancouver one year, to Cleveland the next. The third time up I got thinking, and it suddenly dawned on me there were a lot of players in the N.H.L. to whom I had been superior in the Western and American leagues. I did a careful inventory of my ice behaviour and found the answer—it was a 'slough off' habit. If you take it easy for two or three games in the N.H.L., it's hard to get back into full stride."

To lure stately Jean Beliveau away from the Quebec Aces in 1953, the old Quebec Senior Hockey League was turned pro. His five-year contract reportedly called for $20,000 a year, and, when it expired, the new five-year contract was said to have called for a hoist.

Early in 1963, big Jean entered the ultra-select circle of 300-goal scorers of N.H.L. history (the five others: Rocket Richard, 544; Gordie Howe, 527 at the time; Ted Lindsay, 365; Bernie Geoffrion, 345 at the time; Nels Stewart, 324). But was there ever a doubt that he would hit the peak as a scorer in the major loop?

"Yes, I doubted," Beliveau told me. "In the two seasons before signing with Canadiens, I had scored 123 goals in regular playoff games with the Aces. In a three-game, league-action test with Canadiens, I scored five goals, so I figured my senior hockey tricks would work in the N.H.L. But I soon discovered that it just wasn't so; I was getting checked and the goalers were stopping me too often. I was pretty miserable until I realized that I was making my plays just a bit slow for the N.H.L. and my shot wasn't getting away soon enough to catch the goalers off balance. When I shifted from second to high gear all became O.K."

So, the point was, Beliveau, a scoring giant of senior hockey, had to "speed up" things to score in the N.H.L.—his varied skills remained unchanged but they had to be accelerated.

When Canadiens' Dickie Moore won the N.H.L. scoring championship for the second consecutive season in 1958/59, I reminded him that he had come up twice to the N.H.L. and sent down both times before staying up. I asked what had been his turning point to stardom.

"When Toe Blake took over as coach," replied Moore, "he told me to stop 'fooling around' and shoot more. Then Rocket Richard kept bugging me out on the ice, yelling: 'Shoot, shoot, shoot!' Then he'd bawl me out for not shooting hard enough. When I began shooting oftener and harder my scoring jumped."

When the Ranger fans got "on" Doug Harvey in New York, mate Bathgate explained what happened the night razzing started: "The ice had only been put in the day before and it got cut up in a hurry. That made it difficult to control the puck. Doug doesn't like to give the puck away to the opposition, and he keeps it until he sees a chance to pass. But on that chippy ice in Madison Square Garden he just couldn't do the things he wanted to do with it. But the fans didn't know that."

There's plenty the fans don't know, and plenty they don't see—although they may be looking intently.

I've heard fans gasp, "Boy, is that goaler lucky!" when a hard shot just misses a goal post and hits the boards like a cannon ball. What they didn't realize was that the goalie moved out deliberately to cut down the shooter's angle and probably added a faking move to the "big end" of the net, thus prompting the shooter to try for the short end.

When Bill Durnan won the Vezina (top goalie) Trophy for the sixth time (1949/50), we got yakking about his tricks of the trade. One basic tip, he told me, was to concentrate on worrying about the "soft shots."

"They are the ones that make the difference between a good goaler or just another goaler," said Bill. "In the big moments of hockey games, when an opposing star gets in all alone on a breakaway, any goaler may rise to the crisis with a frantic, successful save. But the same goaler could have lost the game a period earlier by relaxing on what seemed an easy shot."

On the matter of taking chances: "Some youngsters figure it's useless to take chances except in games. That's wrong: chances have to be taken in practices or the young goalie will cultivate the habit of playing all shots 'safe.' It's been my experience that the average shot in practice is harder than what you meet in a game because, in practices, players are not as keyed up and anxious, so they take their time and lean on the drive. Try for them all and risk injury if necessary—it gives confidence for the games."

I asked him how big a role luck plays in goalkeeping, since articles have rated luck as high as fifty per cent. This was Bill's reply: "Goaling is an art calling for a lot of hard training and learning from mistakes; if it wasn't any player could don pads and do just as well as regular goalers."

Next time you spot a lone defenceman stopping a breakaway by two crack forwards, you might see a lot more than luck about it. In practices, he has drilled himself hundreds of times for just such a situation.

The defenceman usually backs up at considerable speed (skating backwards is a regular drill with him) and aims at keeping between the two forwards because a pass can go only one way—if the puck-carrier decides to pass. As the forwards close in, there comes a point when the puck-carrier has to make his play—either pass or carry. At that point the defenceman will likely resort to poke-checking; bodychecking would take him out of the play if his target flipped a pass just as the defenceman threw his check.

I have heard fans comment on the dazzling displays of Rocket Richard and yet convey the impression that he was something of a glorified animal to whom extraordinary physical feats come naturally. Was there nothing else behind the Rocket's skills? I have watched him in, I suppose, four hundred practices as well as some six hundred regular and playoff games. In the games I marvelled at the explosive spurts that would take him from cruising speed to high speed in three or four strides to nab a hard pass and keep going—leaving his cover far behind. In the practices I saw him working on change of pace, deliberately skating sort of lazy-like until the pass was about to be fired. The pass had to "lead" him by a healthy margin, and it had to be fast. In games it often looked almost effortless, but so does ballet by the time it gets through rehearsals.

A junior executive of the House of Seagram recently asked young Charles Bronfman, the President: "What's the easiest way to make a lot of money quickly and legally?"

Bronfman replied: "Inherit."

I suppose the easiest way to dismiss the Brawn versus Brains debate regarding N.H.L. players is to say they must have inherited a lot of brawn and varying supplies of brain from sturdy stock. But the twin heritages have to be put together by the player in the rarefied air of a hockey stratosphere, where no more than one hundred and twenty may be seen in any season from a nation of 143,000 players.

Make no mistake about this brawn and brain business. In hockey, as in love and marriage, you can't have one without the other.

CHAPTER SIX

Please, Pop, Why Did the Whistle Blow?

During the lull caused by a goalkeeper injury in Boston, a group of players were discussing problems involving accident insurance coverage in their profession.

Referee Frank Udvari, skating by the group, was asked if referees met any difficulty getting insured? He said he hadn't and only recently took out an extra $5,000 on his legs. Udvari added with a sporty grin: "You know, everything depends on my ability to keep up with you fellows."

One of the players asked: "How did you spend the money?"

One day at *Weekend Magazine* I got a phone call from our publisher, John G. McConnell. His son had become interested in hockey and an Official Rule Book of the National Hockey League had been found. Result: the eighty-three rules (plus a bushel of subsections) proved so baffling that the boss wanted to know: "Where can I get a 'simple' rule book?"

I had to explain there wasn't any such animal—in fact— ha! ha!—the funniest hockey incident ever was caused by a referee "goofing" in the interpretation of Rule 31. (But more about that later.) The boss asked, somewhat acidly, if something shouldn't be done about it?

It proved an intriguing challenge to our staff as well as to President Campbell of the N.H.L., but we did come up with a "condensation" of the rules, a feature that proved a hit with our readers. I have also seen it hanging on the dressing-room walls of three N.H.L. teams which indicates the boiling-down didn't eliminate rule meat.

To be fair, one has to recognize that it's next to impossible to take a set of laws and re-write them authentically and thoroughly into a breezy, vest-pocket edition. One quick example: the "delayed penalty" comes into force when an infraction has been committed by the team not—repeat, not—in possession. The ref doesn't stop the play but repeatedly points at the player to be penalized until completion of the play by the team in possession.

"Completion" is the key word in the rule, and it just can't be left in the raw. For instance, what about a rebound off the opposing goaler? What happens if the puck has accidentally contacted the body of an opposing player? Does that end the continuity of possession? Rule 34 has to dig into the situation fully. No, rebound or accidental contact as described does not mark "completion" of the play; the puck has to come into possession and control of an opposing player or has to be "frozen." (And what's "frozen"? It can happen in many ways, such as the puck sailing over the rink-side into the crowd.)

However, we concentrated purely on simplification—figuring anybody who gets really intrigued can take an advance course later. So we had artist Ben Wilson come up with eleven hilarious illustrations of those offences that cause whistles to blow and players to be banished. They covered, at a glance: fighting, cross-checking, tripping, elbowing, hooking, holding, charging, spearing, high-sticking, butt-ending and boarding.

This left one other prime source of confusion about whistle toots—namely, those that occur when one or more players are offside.

The ice is divided into three zones—defending, neutral and attacking—by two blue lines. There is also the red line across the centre.

President Campbell said the simplest way to have newcomers to hockey enjoy themselves from the start is to tell them not to worry about those lines, that the basic principle is to get that puck through the opposing team and behind the padded fellow between the goal posts.

"I explain," he added, "that the original game had no lines; they were introduced to keep the game from becoming a long-range shooting match and force players to carry the puck more."

To prevent "offside confusion," Campbell suggests that the onlooker think one way because offsides can only happen to the team with the puck. So picture Joe with the puck in his own defending zone. Joe may pass forward to any mate who is not across the red line at mid-ice. If Joe carries the puck over the first blue line, he may then pass to any mate not yet across the far blue line.

Generally speaking a pass-receiver may not precede the puck into the next zone. Nor may mates of the pass-receiver precede him into the next zone, with one exception. At the red line, mates of the pass-receiver may be actually over the red line and anywhere up to the far blue line. (This eliminates many whistles and allows speed to build up going into the attacking zone.) One other important item: the position of skates determines offsides. As long as Joe has one skate on a line, he may reach far ahead (maybe eight feet) to snare a pass legally.

With that much knowledge, Campbell felt, one has acquired enough savvy to enjoy our "basically simple game." Certainly, it's better than just sitting without any appreciation of why whistles blow, seeming to serve no purpose other than interfering with a fast game. And if your wrath rises over what your new appreciation tells you is a bad call, that also serves a purpose. An old Irish friend used to say: "It's better to fight than be lonesome."

I was awakened about three o'clock one morning by a somewhat fuzzy fan talking from a pay phone in a night club with the noisiest band in town. He began in the familiar way:

"Would you settle a hockey argument?" To eliminate lengthy discussion and allow for more sleeping, I told him to fire away. He asked: "Can a player score a goal with a broken stick?" I snorted "Of course not!" He exclaimed: "Good, I win the bet," and hung up.

Sleep wouldn't come. Sure, we see players dropping what's left of a broken stick and either continuing to play without a stick or skating over for a new one. But something was bothering me. I got up and thumbed through my rule book to Rule 46. Subsection (b) reads: "A goalkeeper may continue to play with a broken stick until stoppage of play or until he has been legally provided with a stick."

Very well, then. Leafs are leading 2-1 over Detroit in the last minute. Detroit yanks their goaler for another forward. At the Leafs' goal, Johnny Bower busts his goal stick near the base. With what's left he takes a desperation golf swing at a loose puck which takes off down the ice and into the empty Detroit net. Yup, a goal can be scored with a broken stick.

If I'd known the name of the caller and the night club, I might have tried yelling down the noisy band to apologize for my blooper. However, there was some solace in recalling a classic comedy of errors from a game in Boston on the night of November 8, 1959.

It all started with a penalty shot called by Referee Dalton McArthur. The visiting team was the Chicago Black Hawks. There was no doubt that the situation demanded a penalty shot call. Bruins' Bronco Horvath, currently tied with the idle Canadiens' Geoffrion for league leadership in scoring, had a breakaway when a Hawk stick was thrown. It knocked the puck off Horvath's stick.

Now, the penalty shot is a rather involved rule, but Rule 31 has been clarified a lot since McArthur "goofed." McArthur later admitted to Referee-in-Chief Carl Voss that he had become confused. It was the only penalty shot of the season, so you can see how rare was the call. At the time the "victim" of a thrown stick didn't necessarily have to take the shot—the shooter could be selected by the team captain. Again, there had been an alteration during the previous summer in which the "offended" team became "non-offending." It meant the same, of course, but a referee just can't pause, remove his rule book and peruse it.

Anyway, whatever was in or wasn't in McArthur's confused mind, he skated over to the Chicago bench and ordered the occupants to select a Boston player for the shot against the Chicago goal. The Chicago team was struck dumb with amazement—but not for long. They sensed a "goof" and quickly moved to make the most of it. At this point entered the human element and the comedy sequence. A heated argument actually developed on the Chicago bench over which a Boston player, Larry Leach or Aut Erikson, had the weaker shot. At the time the two players had scored only one goal apiece.

Meanwhile, over in front of the Boston bench, Horvath was flexing his muscles while eagerly awaiting his golden opportunity to take over the N.H.L. scoring lead. The Bruins weren't too interested in what looked like a protest over at the Chicago bench—after all, the Hawks wouldn't be normal if they didn't register some "beef" with the referee.

The Hawks' debating society finally hit an impasse and called upon their goaler, Glenn Hall, to decide, of all things, which Bruin he preferred to shoot on him. Hall picked Leach.

Referee Dalton promptly skated across to the Bruin bench and told Leach to come out and take the shot. Leach, not comprehending in the least what was happening, but figuring there was something in the rule book's fine print he'd missed, got up and skated by the flabbergasted Horvath.

Behind the Bruin bench, coach Milt Schmidt was madly waving a copy of the rule book, but he didn't dare step out on the ice to follow the referee—it would have cost him an automatic $500 fine. Behind Milt was the General Manager, Lynn Patrick and yelling: "Go out, I'll pay your fine!"

McArthur acted firmly and swiftly. He waved Leach toward the puck. Leach swung in, picked it up, shot and Hall turned the puck aside with ease.

It all could have ended unhappily in the hockey court of appeals, but the indignant Bruins went on to win, 5-3. Leach, deeply insulted by being selected as the team's worst shot, fired the first goal and Horvath, even more irked about it all, scored two as well as adding an assist. (P.S. Horvath ended that season second in N.H.L. scoring to Bobby Hull, by a margin of one point.)

The McArthur incident was remarkable in that an indisputable boner by a referee is so rare. Indeed, the referees of the Big Time have in the main proven pretty remarkable fellows.

I have never heard a wide-eyed boy saying he'd like to be a referee when he grows up. I have never heard adult observers envy a referee; comment is usually along the line that "I wouldn't have his job for all the tea in China."

Nobody likes to be unpopular and, judging by even the routine N.H.L. game's arguments, the referee starts and ends the season enveloped in scathing denunciation.

However, things aren't always as they appear out there. The famed Referee "Red" Storey was working Boston Garden one night while Fern Flaman was the bashingest Bruin of them all. Storey handed him a minor penalty, and the two engaged in a nose-to-nose controversy for at least thirty seconds. I fully expected to see an additional ten-minute (misconduct) penalty slapped on Flaman but it wasn't. After the game, curiosity prompted me to query Flaman about what had gone on?

Flaman laughed. "I breathed on Storey, told him I had a severe cold and was glad to give it to him. You know what the big redhead answered? He told me: 'That's the cold I left here two weeks ago and I'm glad you picked it up.' "

Although no player in my memory has ever passed a plaudit

to a ref, I always felt that during his long whistle-blowing career, Storey was a favourite with the players. For one thing, he was a hard-working ref and, for another, he has a spectacular athletic record of his own—highlighted by three touchdowns for Toronto Argos in the last quarter of a Grey Cup game against Winnipeg. The players also made the most of Storey's sense of humour.

I was at a game in Madison Square Garden when Canadiens were the visiting team. Boom Boom Geoffrion drew a minor penalty for high-sticking a Ranger player, and he skated to the sin-bin. The Rangers protested to Referee Storey showing the high-sticking had drawn blood. In accordance with the rules, Storey skated over to the penalty bench, lifted the minor to a major penalty and skated away to face off the puck.

In the press box, we watched in dismay as Geoffrion banged open the door and skated furiously out to Storey, showering the ref with snow as he stopped. There he stood, shaking a gloved finger under Storey's nose, getting off what had been on his chest. Then Geoffrion wheeled, returned to the penalty bench and sat down in an air of triumph while the New York crowed howled things like: "What's the matter, Storey? Letting him get away with it? So Canadiens run the league, eh, Storey?"

On leaving the Garden I ran into Red and we found a quick spot for a cold beer. Eventually, I recalled the Geoffrion incident and expressed surprise that Storey had ignored the public berating act.

Storey howled with laughter. "Can you guess what that comedian said to me while he was finger-wagging under my nose? Boom said: 'I just came out, Red, to tell you I won't hold this against you.' "

After a lusty quaff, Red added: "That howling crowd tempted me to slap a misconduct on Geoffrion for coming out but I was afraid I'd bust out laughing as I did so."

The major hockey referee has to be something apart.

Because a man has been a star in the league, it doesn't mean he can be a good referee. I saw one such ex-star on trial one night become so befuddled he actually paused to ask rinkside fans for an opinion on something that had just happened.

The referee has to know the complex book of rules so thoroughly that as a situation occurs his mind is almost an automatic filing case that pops open at the exact spot with the correct ruling.

A few seasons ago, again it was in Boston, Bruin Jerry Toppazzini streaked in on right wing and fired from a difficult angle at the Chicago net. Goalie Glenn Hall made a motion but didn't touch the puck which ended in the corner of the rink. Play continued down the ice and was well beyond mid-ice when referee Matt Pavelich blew his whistle.

"That should have been a goal back there," he announced, "the puck went right through the net."

Naturally there was an uproar. The goal judge hadn't turned on his light. And why hadn't Matt stopped the game when it happened, instead of twenty seconds later?

Matt was perfectly frank. "Sorry, boys, as I skated down the ice I got thinking."

Everybody skated back to the Chicago net. Sure enough, there was a hole in the netting just about where Matt thought there should be. What escaped everybody at the moment was the inherent honesty that made Matt risk looking inefficient, if not plain silly, should a hole not be found.

In one of the earlier games handled by Bill Chadwick, the all-time great N.H.L. referee was working in Madison Square Garden before a capacity crowd. Goalie Chuck Rayner, in the net for New York Rangers, reached for and caught a blistering shot from short range by Canadiens' Rocket Richard. Rayner swooped his glove hand upwards in what appeared to be a triumphal gesture which the crowd uproariously cheered. Not many goalers were stopping leaned-on shots from close-in by the Rocket in those days.

Suddenly the tumult came to a disbelieving halt. There was Referee Chadwick, alongside the net, signalling a goal, although no red goal light was showing. Chadwick ruled that the force of the puck had driven Rayner's hand back over the goal line (the puck has to be competely across it) but he had immediately swooped his hand upwards to "establish a save."

Aside from the courage of the referee to make such a call against the home team, an impressive fact was missed. Chadwick had been up there, in line with the goal, ahead of a speedster such as the Rocket. And referees have to stay out there throughout the game—they get no relieving shifts.

Everybody else in the joint is apparently allowed to lose his or her head, but not the man with the whistle. Even when he gets socked flush on the jaw—the N.H.L. President Campbell actually was, in his pre-war officiating days, by Bruins' giant Dit Clapper.

A veteran of one hundred and fifty-five scheduled and twelve playoff games, Campbell was working in a torrid, 1937 Bruins-Maroons Stanley Cup playoff game. In those days the referee was the lone official on the ice and when, with four minutes to go, Clapper and Maroons' Dave Trottier began mixing it, Campbell rushed in between them. Clapper's fist landed squarely and Campbell's knees rocked.

When Campbell handed Clapper a major penalty (not even a match penalty), the Montreal press howled for his scalp—was Boston running the league? Years later, Campbell told me: "The game had been a severe one and Clapper was, I knew, worked up. I frankly doubted if he knew where the punch was going, and with fans paying to see players, not referees, why not give him the benefit of the doubt? Anyway, with only four minutes to go, a major would keep him out of the rest of the game anyway."

The courage of these strictly select and unsung heroes of hockey's Big Time has always impressed me. There are the brave debunkers who charge ice brawls are phoney. I usually refer them to Ace Bailey, of the Toronto Maple Leafs, who hovered near death after a tangle with Boston's Eddie Shore. If the debunkers say this was "more accidental than deliberate," I suggest they ask "Wild Bill" Ezinicki, now a golf pro in the United States.

Ezinicki, then with Boston, and Ted Lindsay, then with Detroit, were getting along just peachy until Lindsay gave Ezinicki a shove. Ezinicki replied with a one-stitch cut on Lindsay's forehead. Lindsay retaliated with an eleven-stitch bang on Ezinicki's nogging. Ezinicki tore loose from restraining hands, ran into a Lindsay right hook and crashed backwards on the ice with such force that he picked up four more stitches on the back of the head as well as four more on the front of his already battered puss. He also lost a tooth. Ezzy's nineteen stitches and missing molar cost Lindsay a $300 fine, plus a three-game suspension without pay.

Call those fights anything you like—but not phoney. They are to be deplored, but physical-contact games, played at such speed with be-padded muscles and wooden sticks, do explode at times. And the officials are expected to handle the situations.

Cooper Smeaton, senior trustee of the Stanley Cup, was a pioneer referee in the N.H.L. He toted the whistle at the first games in Chicago and New York as well as at many dozens of major games before that—working alone on the ice and facing perennial fists or threats off the ice.

Cooper is one of the four referees listed in the Hockey Hall of Fame (others are Mike Rodden, Mickey Ion and Chaucer Elliott), which strikes me as fitting recognition of what those old-timers contributed in the raw-meat era of the game when, on reading back, it's almost incomprehensible that any order could come out of the chaotic violence.

Newsy Lalonde still looks back with awe upon damage wrought in Calgary one night while Cully Wilson (later Toronto St. Pats) was the terror of Western hockey: "Cully had cross-checked Dick Irvin's lower teeth right into his tongue and was handed a major penalty. But that wasn't enough in Dick's opinion. Dick manoeuvred near enough to the penalty box to pole-axe the sitting Cully unconscious. Cully had enough stitches to weave an Indian blanket."

Referees, alone then and with aides now, have played a vital role in bringing the game along. It's a game of violence which permits physical contact at high speeds among men carrying padded muscles and hard sticks. Do missile-throwing nitwits in the stands ever pause to reflect on how weak hockey would be without the strength of efficient and courageous refereeing?

I went to Frank Udvari, senior referee of the N.H.L., with the question: "What do you think of the fans whose prime purpose in life seems to boo you?"

Veteran of some 1,500 pro games and 600 of them as ref in regular or playoff N.H.L. games, Udvari claims he has to be grateful to them for helping provide a well-paid (about $13,500 per year) career in major hockey. "But," he adds, "I have to say that fans who boo N.H.L. referees seldom seem to know what they are booing about."

Udvari pulled out his well-thumbed rules book and stopped at Rule 62 to read aloud: "A minor penalty shall be imposed on a player who interferes with or impedes the progress of an opponent who is not in possession of the puck...."

He lowered the book. "What fans often fail to realize is that a defending player is allowed to 'shadow' an intending pass-receiver closely and stride for stride. It often happens that they get snarled—one brings the other down. If the referee judges it was accidental, there is no penalty to be called."

And it's mainly around the goal areas that booers "see" most illegal interference.

"But once again, is it really what it seems?" asks Udvari. "A defenceman is allowed to 'stand his ground'—he is not required to get out of the way of any attacking player. On the other hand, an attacking player may be jockeying around so furiously in front of the net, hoping to deflect a shot into the net, that home fans think he is being interfered with. Actually, it's a question of who's interfering with whom."

Sure, Rule 45, allows a minor or major penalty to be given a player at the discretion of the referee who causes an opponent to be thrown violently into the boards.

"But the word discretion is significant," says Udvari. "The noise factor often over-influences fans. Some players have developed a noise art by smashing their stick into the boards and making with pained gestures. However, the noise and amount of protection given by modern equipment makes most board clashes vastly less violent than they seem."

Anyway, he stresses, it's quite legal (how many fans know this one?) for a defending player to "ride" a puck-carrier into the boards while going parallel with him? On the other hand, a defending player who "lines up" an opponent and reefs him into the boards is sure bait for the sin-bin.

And how often, how very often, have you seen a defender trip a puck-carrier and the blankety-blank referee ignore it? Udvari agrees but flips to Rule 82 which bans tripping.

"I would say that we referees, despite the booers, catch almost one hundred per cent of the tripping offences because we follow the puck—it's the illegal interference behind our backs or down at the far end of the rink we admittedly miss but tripping, no.

"What, almost invariably, the booer doesn't realize is that if a defender hook-checks a puck-carrier, knocks the puck away and, in so doing, trips him, it's legal. But if the puck is so far ahead of the defender that he can't reach it, yet he tries a hook-check that trips, he's out."

All of this won't, I know, change the chronic booer and/or missile-tosser. He is usually a hen-pecked husband or a brow-beaten employee relieving a frustration. It's either the rink or the psychiatrist's couch for him. The rink is more pleasant.

CHAPTER SEVEN

Yes, Junior, Coaches have Mothers, Too

While Rudy Pilous was coaching Chicago he often used a story for putting across a point. During a practice, while he was taking his third-place team all the way to the 1961 Stanley Cup, I heard him "illustrating" for any players and press who would listen how "constant alertness pays off."

It appears that while the late Marilyn Monroe was working out details of divorce from Joe DiMaggio, she walked one day into a New York lawyer's office with the lawyer's wife. Marilyn looked like a dream, the lawyer's wife like a nightmare.

After they left, a new office boy entered the lawyer's office, sniffed and exclaimed "Geez, it smells good, sir!"

The lawyer also took an appreciative sniff. "That perfume belonged to Marilyn Monroe—the girl who was with my wife."

The tactful kid came back: "Sir, which was Miss Monroe?"

The lawyer studied the kid for a long, solemn moment, then said: "Here's five bucks, son. In a couple of years I want you to remember how generous your old boss was—and throw a little of your business my way."

In a serious vein, the same Pilous used many unusual wrinkles that indicate there is more to Big Time coaching than meets the fan's eye. One of his pet stunts, when the Hawks weren't checking, is one he developed while coaching junior hockey— and "it still works when hockey players grow up and, like a pro golfer, forget a fundamental without appreciating what's happened."

73

Pilous forms two teams on the ice and allows one team only two sticks, carried by goaler and centre.

It's almost unbelievable how seldom the fully equipped team scores. Pilous' point, of course, is to impress on players how they can check if they concentrate on checking.

One morning in the Detroit Olympia, watching Red Wings practice, I learned the technique behind the apparently foolhardy and matter-of-luck business of a defenceman going down on his knees directly in front of (and facing) an opponent in the act of shooting.

The trick is to watch the puck-carrier's eyes. He'll drop his eyes to the puck just before shooting—to make sure the puck is cuddled on the right spot of the blade, not too far up or back. When his eyes drop, you start to drop, too—not before, because if you drop too soon the puck-carrier may veer around you instead of shooting, leaving you saying your prayers on lonely ice.

But now for the sequel, courtesy of Coach Sid Abel of the Wings: "We try to get our forwards into the habit of lifting their eyes for a quick peek after lowering them for the shot, just hoping the opposing defenceman has been deked into falling early."

At a Canadiens' practice, with the maddening throng absent from the Montreal Forum, don't be surprised if you hear Coach "Toe" Blake ordering some of his famed scorers to "forget the opposing net."

He explained: "Most fans judge a forward by his scoring. But if his opposing covers have totalled as much as he has, the over-all result is poor. Top-scoring lines are often the most scored against as well: in 1959/60 we ended first, yet the tail-end Rangers were the only team to break even with us in the fourteen times we met. Meaning only one thing: we let down defensively against Rangers."

Blake adds: "Sometimes when a line isn't doing well

74

defensively it's not their fault. Maybe it's the coach's in not putting players who jell on the same line."

In 1960/61, forward Gilles Tremblay played forty-five regular games with the Canadiens, during which he scored seven goals and was credited with eleven assists. The next season, 1961/62, he exploded as a scorer with thirty-two goals, twenty-two assists in seventy games. "What happened?" the fans asked, because while many are called to the N.H.L., only a chosen few become trigger-pullers.

The only logical answer—since Gilles didn't seem to change his style—lay in Coach Blake's constant harping on one point in practice. He kept telling Gilles to hold his stick lower (instead of carrying it waist-high) in front of the opposing goal. In this way he was better able to respond with split-second reaction on tipping, deflecting or intercepting any pucks whizzing within his range.

At Maple Leaf Gardens in Toronto you are bound to hear Coach "Punch" Imlach harping on positional hockey. Certainly he's made it pay off. For the two seasons before he took over the Leafs in 1958/59, the team (it's hard to believe) had ended out of the playoffs, didn't have a player among the Top Ten in scoring or a player on either the first or second All-Star teams.

Punch preaches: "The advantages of playing positional hockey on the offensive lie in providing an organized attack. Defensively, it works to your advantage when the puck suddenly changes possession and you're left in better position to catch the player you are assigned to cover."

Back in 1952, when Imlach was coaching Quebec Aces, I went to do a feature on a promising young hockey player under his wing by the name of Jean Beliveau. I still recall Imlach telling his charges: "Never give up when chasing a puck-carrier—most of them slow up at the opposing blue line, and if you haven't slowed up, chances are you'll catch him."

It's doubtful whether any coach in any other sport is called upon for the mental alertness and quick decisions an N.H.L. coach faces. Football and baseball pilots, for instance, work from stationary starts, but the hockey mentor is forced to make moves on the fly.

Probably the best example in that category involved the late Dick Irvin while coaching Canadiens in the final game of the 1952/53 season. It was at Detroit and it was a "nothing" game (that is, it couldn't affect the standings), with the spotlight centred exclusively on Red Wings' Gordie Howe who had forty-nine goals already scored and needed only one to tie or two to beat the all-time seasonal record of fifty then held alone by Rocket Richard.

Before leaving Montreal, the publicity wise Irvin announced that he would shift the Rocket from right to left wing to cover Howe personally. It sounded like a good idea—in Montreal. But when Irvin entered the dressing room in Detroit, his heart sank. After nine years with the Rocket, he had grown to recognize signs of an impending explosion. And Richard was sitting there, dour and ominous. In recent rhubarbs with referees he had shown signs of tension build-up as the season was ending, and now, with the prospect of losing his cherished "50" record....

Irvin was in a dilemma. If a row broke out in this "nothing" game, it could mean loss through suspension of the Rocket for the playoffs—and loss of the Stanley Cup for the Canadiens. On the other hand, if he didn't play Richard, and Howe broke the record, wouldn't it affect the morale of not only the Rocket but the entire team?

Irvin decided to play the Rocket.

Sure enough, within minutes Rocket caught Howe with a bodycheck and draped the mightiest Red Wing of them all over the boards. The crowd howled for blood. Irvin told me later of his quick decision at that point: "I ordered Rocket to lay off Howe and told Bert Olmstead and Johnny McCormack to concentrate on Howe regardless of the game's outcome. I even had Olmstead escort Howe to the Detroit bench on player changes just to get him riled. Yet so rapidly do the lines tumble over the boards in modern hockey that I'd lose track; it seemed every time I looked up the Rocket was hell-benting for Howe again. Somehow, the game ended in one piece. It was a tie but I didn't care.

"The big thing was that Howe had been held scoreless with only one shot on goal, and Rocket was yipping around the room—happy as a kid. I knew then we couldn't be beaten all the way to the world championship."

Three seasons later the same Irvin was coaching the Black Hawks and the same Rocket ran wild in Chicago, scoring three goals. I found it hard to keep my face straight when, in the post-mortem after the debacle, a Chicago writer expressed surprise that Irvin, of all people, didn't have the Rocket "taped." Why, he asked Irvin, hadn't he produced strategy to stop the Rocket?

"Because this isn't baseball," snapped Irvin. "In hockey you can't walk the big batters."

In the second game of the 1963 Leafs-Canadiens playoff semi-finals, the score was 3-2 for Leafs, with a little over a minute to go. The Canadiens put on the big pressure, had an offside goal called back but kept pressing.

With one minute to go, Coach Imlach sent out a Leaf forward line made up entirely of centres: Dave Keon, Red Kelly and Bobby Pulford. The idea was, of course, that centres are usually better defensively than other forwards. It worked; Canadiens were held. Afterwards, Imlach shrugged his move off with: "Necessity is the mother of invention."

But where did he get the idea? I have never seen the move made before, never heard of it being done, yet it was so logical, one wonders why it was new. It was also a gem example

77

of what a coach can do to help even a team then reigning as world champs.

While on the subject of hockey strategy, I felt a genuine pang for Canada's goalie, Denis Brodeur, one day during the 1956 Winter Olympics at Cortina d'Ampezzo, when the Russians turned up unexpectedly at a practice to watch our team.

Brodeur was sprawling to stop a screened shot that seemed to be coming in fairly low from right wing. It was a little higher than he thought and the puck bounced off the top of his hairy head. Mindful of his audience, Brodeur didn't even rub the spot as he leapt back to his feet, smiling cheerily.

It gave Coach Bobby Bauer, the ex-Boston Bruin star, an idea. He quietly passed word for all the Canadians to keep shooting at Brodeur's head. When the practice ended, Brodeur stomped into the room raging mad. He threw his stick at the wall and roared:

"What-in-hell was the big idea out there?"

"I told the boys to do it," placated Bauer, "just to give the Russian goalie something to think about."

"The Russian goalie?" rasped Brodeur, "what about your own goalie?"

Bauer made a grand gesture out of a shrug. "What have we got to worry about with a good spare goaler like Keith Woodall?"

Another producer of prime prose among Canadian coaches was Wren Blair, head man of the Whitby Dunlops at the World Tournament in Oslo, Norway, in 1958.

He emerged from the Jordal Amfi rink, blowing fuses into the sub-zero air despite having registered a 10-2 win over Sweden. He was promptly surrounded by the Swedish press.

"Tonight's refereeing was a disgrace," beefed Blair, "if my boys can give their best out there, why can't the refs? Tomorrow I intend to call up president Bunny Ahearne of the International Ice Hockey Federation and—"

"Do you intend to protest the game?" pressed an eager Swede.

Blair paused to glare at the newsman. "You knucklehead," he replied, "how could I protest a 10-2 win?"

It was the same Blair who, in a pre-series exhibition game at Stockholm, awed the press by complaining over lack of penalties given against his own team.

The Whitby team had already piled up a 10-0 lead and Blair was getting bored. Noting that the refs were concentrating on offsides, fighting and boarding, he decided on an experiment. Blair told Ted O'Connor to hand No. 11 of the Swedish national team a butt-end.

By Canadian standards it wasn't much of a butt-end, but No. 11 went down in a dramatic dying-swan routine. Both refs gathered, staring down at the moaning player but nothing happened to O'Connor.

"Those refs," exclaimed Blair in disgust, "must think No. 11 had a heart attack."

At the end of the second period, Blair made a personal appeal on behalf of clean hockey to one of the refs, Toni Neumaier of Germany, who could speak some English.

"It makes no difference to me what you fellows do," said Blair, "we're going to win 15-0 anyway. But if you don't give penalties, how are we going to get practise against the power play?"

Referee Neumaier glowered at Blair, saying "You play too rough," and skated away.

Both the Russians and the Canadians were quartered in the Viking Hotel in Oslo during the tourney. The Russians proved the handshakingest team the Whitby Dunnies had ever encountered and real bone crushers at that. It now developed into psychological warfare and, so help me, assistant coach Ed Redmond called a special strategic session to instruct in counter-attack. It was quite a sight to see the Canadian players shaking and re-shaking one another's hands as Redmond instructed: "Grip first and firm. . .no, it needn't be too hard but it's impossible for the Russians to apply a bone-crusher on a firm grip. In this way you will instil a feeling of futility in them."

Of course, strategy is a many splendoured thing in hockey. But I suppose we writers and commentators often read strategy into a situation that merely happened. A star player does a lot of things instinctively that the best-laid plans of mice and men could never pull off.

King Clancy recalls a conversation he had after being traded by the Ottawa Senators to the Toronto Leafs. Conn Smythe, then managing the Leafs, remarked that Ottawa never seemed to have any trouble with the Rangers' line, made up of the Cook brothers and Frank Boucher, whereas the trio used to treat the Leafs as if it were a practice.

"I want you to tell me what strategy Ottawa used," said Smythe.

Clancy confessed he didn't know what Smythe was talking about and, rather lamely, suggested Ottawa was just lucky against Rangers. Smythe wasn't satisfied and pointed out that Rangers appeared able to get a lot of direct shots on the Leafs' goal but that they didn't against Ottawa.

When Leafs played Rangers the next time, Clancy automatically did just what he had always done while with Ottawa: "I stood in front of the goal."

He had quite a night, intercepting a lot of passes and preventing the big line from getting a single direct shot on goal. After the game, Smythe came up to Clancy with an outstretched hand.

"Plenty foxy, King, plenty foxy," he said, "pretending you had no plan for playing that line."

Today Clancy admits: "I'm glad Conn noticed it because I didn't know I'd been using any strategy. I was just doing what I thought best."

In the 1958 Stanley Cup finals, Canadiens polished off Bruins in six games—the cincher being a 5-3 win in Boston. A scribe asked the Bruin general manager, Lynn Patrick, what had been the turning point in the game.

"When they dropped the puck for the opening faceoff," replied Patrick.

However, despite a tendency to exaggerate strategy in headline hockey, more strategy is used than the casual onlooker ever sees. But don't feel too badly about not seeing it—even coaches get puzzled over the obvious, just as Conn Smythe was once puzzled.

One night in Oslo the Norwegian coach approached me with an interpreter to ask if it were usual in Canada to do as the Whitby team was doing in sending two players in to forecheck a puck-carrier in the latter's zone? To the Norwegian it looked like a waste of one player and downright dangerous.

Rather flattered, I suppose, I told him the play was used by a lot of top-ranking teams. The first forechecker aims to circle the puck-carrier into the other forechecker. The third member of the defending forward line is left back to intercept a long pass; meanwhile his defence moves up behind him.

The next night, with pangs of conscience, I saw Norway using the same play against Canada—luckily without much polish. Afterwards I confessed to Wren Blair that I'd spouted "vital information to the enemy." But Blair told me to go in peace, recalling the reply of Hangman Ellis when asked in Regina if he used any set plan in his work. "Plans are simple to devise," replied the remarkably erudite Hangman Ellis, "it's how you execute them that counts."

I think the modern crop of coaches represents the smartest array on a six-team basis I have ever known, but it would be difficult to supplant Dick Irvin as the shrewdest the game has seen.

He used to sigh over his mail: "It's amazing how many

unemployed National Hockey League coaches there are around town but, after more than twenty years of handling teams in this league, I have yet to meet the one grandstand coach I'm really looking for."

"And who would that be, Dick?" somebody asked.

"The guy who can tell me what to do before a game and not after it's over."

One letter came from a chap who wanted a few tips on how to be a successful coach. Irvin showed me his letter in reply: "The best tip of all is to get yourself some good hockey players."

Without them no coach can get anywhere. With them a poor coach can still lose, but a good coach can make good players "jell" as a team and improve as a team.

"As I have seen my job with great Canadien teams," said Irvin, "it lay in figuring the opposing team's strength and concentrating what I had against it. This means altering our defence against various styles of attack, and our attack against various styles of defence. Above all, abstain from rigidity; if you've broken up a line and results aren't as good as formerly, reunite them immediately rather than try to vindicate your first decision."

There's another memorable point I learned from Irvin during fascinating hours on trains. I pass it on to new coaches of the future N.H.L. "When you get to be coach in the Big Time, you have to take players as they come. There is little hope of changing them after they've 'arrived.' The coach who thinks he can remould players is due for hard times. The only approach is to take what you have and adapt your attack and defence accordingly."

Years later, early in the 1962/63 season, I recalled this sage advice during an interview with Coach Rudy Pilous at Chicago. He had a batch of statistical reports in front of him. His team wasn't cooking.

"Look at Bobby Hull, for example," complained Rudy, "he's had thirty-three shots on goal so far this season and only one lousy goal. It's excessive use of the damn slapshot that's causing it, I know."

"Well then," I injected, "why don't you, as coach, order him to cut down on his slapshooting?"

Rudy dropped his charts and glowered at me from under those bushy eyebrows. "Last season Hull won the scoring championship, tied the record of fifty goals in a season of which he claims half of them came from the slapshot. Do you think that I, as coach, dare to tell Hull how to shoot?"

Nor is there much a coach can do about an N.H.L. goaler— the breed is both rare and extremely valuable. You can't use the whip on a goaler, you can't tell him how to goal. You may be able to detect signs of breakdown when nerves blow, as I've seen with three of them, and work hard with the psychology.

Few fans really appreciate the magnitude of mental strain on the fella between the goal posts. After Canadiens' Jacques Plante won the Vezina Trophy for the sixth time in 1962, I got fed up on fans who snorted: "But who couldn't be top goalie with such teams as Plante has ahead of him?"

So I did some digging. Plante had then been in five hundred and eighty-five regular and playoff games, which represented a total of some seventeen thousand five hundred stops. (By a stop is meant a puck that would have gone into the net except for the goaler stopping it; not included are pucks which just miss the side of the net even though the goalie has deliberately cut off the shooter's angle and caused him to miss.)

Now, since top scorers get more shots on goal than other players, one has to recognize it took a lot of science as well as luck to make seventeen thousand five hundred stops off N.H.L. shooters. But how many could be labelled as really—but really —"dangerous"?

Let's omit long shots—although many bouncers cause frantic moments. Omit, too casual rubber from which most steam has been removed by a blocking mate, and routine shots off routine players. My estimate is that even the harshest estimate would have to regard one out of five shots as dangerous.

So, by the time Plante had nailed down his sixth Vezina, he had "robbed" opponents of at least three thousand five hundred goals.

No, coaches just couldn't teach anybody on how to do that.

There's one thing common to all N.H.L. coaches I have known—an element of tough-mindedness. Dick Irvin was the first to forbid players from helping injured mates off the ice: "It encourages too much Sarah Bernhardt stuff out there."

Glenn Harmon, the old Canadien, still tells of an incident in which rock-ribbed Kenny Reardon (now Vice-President of the Club) was the victim of Irvin's regulation.

"While Bill Ezinicki was playing with Boston," says Harmon, "he developed a pet play in which he'd circle his own defence and catch an opposing puck-carrier circling from the far side of the defence.

"We were playing in Boston and Reardon came down in a mad rush. He was off-balance, circling, head-down, one knee bent and frantically concentrating on retaining possession of the puck when Ezzy caught Kenny with what we used to call 'the Ezinicki Iron Shoulder Pad'—a regular shoulder pad reinforced with tape.

"Ezzy's shoulder caught Kenny squarely on the jaw. Kenny went down with a crash, rolled over, lurched unsteadily to his knees then to his skates. Nobody dared assist as he made for the Canadien bench. His legs were so wobbly he looked like he was giving one of those comic drunk routines. His eyes were actually crossed. All of us on the bench howled with laughter at the sight."

84

Gordie Howe (9), Detroit star and an all-time great, runs into a spot of trouble with Toronto goalie Johnny Bower during 1963 Stanley Cup finals.

At home, Gordie runs into more trouble from young sons who show no awe over their father's hardrock reputation in the N.H.L. wars.

Michael Burns   Alexandra Stud

Referee Frank Udvari (2) illustrates how modern officials must stay "on top" of sizzling action. In rear, "Red" Kelly, M.P., checks on Udvari.

Ref's problem: if he watches puck being shoved aside by Ranger goalie "Gump" Worsley, he misses Doug Harvey holding Leaf George Armstrong (10).

This coaching tough-mindedness explains the eruptions of coaches—such as the "Little Eva" crossing of the Chicago Ice by Toe Blake in the 1961 semi-final playoffs to sock the referee (at a cost of a $2,000 fine). There was no justification for the action, but Blake has always fought as hard at being a coach as he did as a player. So it was understandable and, in my opinion, a sort of misdirected assurance to the paying fan that he is seeing all-out hockey effort.

"Fiery" Phil Watson was a battler as a player. He didn't change as coach. His running feud with popular goalie "Gump" Worsley in the Rangers' camp made a stack of headlines. But even Gump paid tribute to Watson's encyclopaedic mind: "I've never seen anything like it—he not only can recall every play of the last game, like he was reading a movie out loud, but also every play in which you goofed last season or seasons before. I never argued with Phil about games."

Shortly before noon on the day of a Rangers game in Montreal, Watson phoned me to say he was "all stuffed up" with a cold and would I get him into the health room at the Montreal Amateur Athletic Association for a session in the steam room? I did so gladly and, after the steam, we stretched out on adjacent cots under the big sunlamp. We dozed off for a while and Phil left, thanking me profusely.

That night the Rangers took an awful shellacking at the Forum. After the game I accompanied other Montreal writers into their room. Watson saw us entering from the far side and bellowed: "Throw those damn Montreal writers out of here!"

"But, Phil," I couldn't resist yelling back, "only at noon today we slept together. . . ."

Watson fumed anew: "I was better with my cold—get out, I said!"

Even at that I got off easy. Take what happened to Lew

Walter, Detroit *Times* hockey writer and former American college grid star.

Herb Goren, now publicity chief of the Rangers, was writing for the *New York Sun* when the Chicago Hawks were deep down in the cellar and then coached by Charley Conacher, ex-Leaf and one of the toughest hunks of ice-star in N.H.L. history.

Goren heard that some Hawks were vigorously unhappy over Conacher calling practices at 1:00 a.m., the only time ice was available at Chicago. He wrote a "dissension" story which was picked up by the news services and relayed to Detroit where the Hawks had just dropped a 9-2 decision.

Lew Walter dropped into the Hawks' room and asked what he thought was a routine question: "Is it true, Charley, that there's dissension on your team?"

Conacher came up from the floor with a right that flattened Walter. (Lawyers got into the act later.) "That was the wildest haymaker punch ever thrown," reflects Goren today. "It was really aimed at me in New York."

We of the press box have always preached that coaches should "be able to take it" publicity-wise but, in all fairness and despite any evidence to the contrary, they are only human—yes, junior, coaches have mothers, too.

Even Dick Irvin used to go into Greta Garbo "wanna be alone" sulks during losing streaks. One afternoon, during the long train trek back to Montreal from Chicago, he sat back among the press to rap his critics.

"For decades I was the target of press questions and problems," he said, "then came radio and then television. It's become difficult to keep from going completely crackers during the long season. Let me give you a case in point.

"On a recent trip to Detroit, where we leave Montreal at eleven p.m. and get in early next afternoon, I sat up with the press boys until 2:30 a.m. When a card game started I got up, walked twenty feet to my compartment, went to bed, got up the next morning at ten o'clock, shaved, dressed and walked back the twenty feet to where the card game was still going strong. One of the press boys looked up and asked: 'What's new, Dick?''

What keeps coaches in the punishing profession?

Even they don't seem too sure. After Phil Watson was fired by Rangers while in hospital having his ulcers removed, he took over the Boston Bruins and eventually got fired there, too. But somehow he retained enough sense of humour to regale the press with a story about two former hockey coaches meeting on the street.

Said the first: "I've been out of work two years."

"And I've been out for five years," sighed the other, "You know, sometimes I think I'm getting out of this business."

CHAPTER EIGHT

Hockey Fans Should Be Heard and Not Seen

It was nearing three a.m. in Detroit on April 6, 1955. Canadiens had taken an awful 7-1 beating in a playoff with Red Wings a few hours previously at the Olympia. I was walking through the railway station with Doug Harvey, then a Canadien, wrapped in gloomy contemplation.

He nudged me with an elbow and pointed toward a stack of early-morning newspapers just planked down by the newsstand. The headline read: "Prime Minister Churchill Resigns."

"There," said Harvey, "is a fan who really takes it hard."

The care and feeding of the modern hockey fan is getting to be quite a problem—what with just under three million of them paying for the right to create holler and havoc during 1962/63 regular and playoff games alone.

I was left temporarily blinded by a tear-gas bomb thrown by a fan in the Richard Riot of 1955. I've had the sleeve of my topcoat torn off in New York. In 1951, after doing what I thought to be a bright and breezy feature on hockey in the raw at Glace Bay, Nova Scotia, Mayor D. A. MacDonald wrote my editor under the town seal to say that my article had been widely read by the fans and that there were two schools of thought.

"One maintains that O'Brien is an inane, ill-informed, gullible ignoramus," wrote His Worship. "The other is that he is a cold, calculating, selfish opportunist who would resort to ridicule, exaggeration and downright falsehoods. . . ."

88

When a friendly-looking fellow handed me a folded paper one night in Detroit for what I thought was my autograph (yeah, there are fans who collect sportwriters' monikers) I graciously took it. As he walked away whistling I looked puzzledly at the paper—it was a subpoena notifying me of a $250,000 libel action being taken jointly by the Detroit club and some of its personnel over a column I had written in the old *Montreal Standard*.

(The press boys had a field day. The prize comment was made by Baz O'Meara in the *Montreal Star* with: "If O'Brien goes for the bundle on this one he will be practically bankrupt.")

No-o-o, I can't say I like looking at hockey fans any more—even those howling pictures of them scare me to death. But they do make wonderful listening.

For many a hockey moon—as playing star, referee and coach —Frank "King" Clancy fought against a tendency toward "rabbit ears" with regard to taunts from the fans. But one night in 1953, while behind the Maple Leafs' bench as coach during a game in Boston, his curiosity was aroused during a quiet moment by a foghorn voice from the first gallery.

"Hey, Clancy!" the fan had bellowed, "didja know we've got a town twenty miles out of Boston named after you?"

Clancy looked up: "What town is that?"

The foghorn bellowed back: "Marblehead!"

Ranger publicist Herb Goren tells of the night in Madison Square Garden when Oscar Levant, noted pianist and ardent hockey fan, was being bugged by a woman in the next box who persisted in ignoring the game to talk music. Finally she leaned over in the lull that followed a 3-0 goal scored against Rangers and asked in a loud, confidential whisper: "Mr. Levant, what inspired you to take up the piano as a career?"

Levant gazed deliberately to right, to left, then replied, in an even louder whisper: "Because my beer glass used to fall off the end of my violin."

After Rocket Richard scored his 70th goal in playoff action during the 1957 series, a chartered accountant wrote me to say how lucky Senator Donat Raymond (then president of Canadiens) was in signing the Rocket. Wrote the busy accountant:

"If the Rocket had insisted that his contract include a bonus of one, just one, cent for his first Stanley Cup goal with said bonus to be doubled with each subsequent goal [that is, two cents, four cents, eight cents, etc.] last night's 70th goal would have cost the Senator just under three billions of billions of dollars or, to be exact $2,951,479,051,793,528,258.56."

Back in the late '20's, while Montreal Maroons were still in existence, Elmer Ferguson, now a columnist with the *Montreal Star*, was acting as penalty timekeeper during a particularly violent game at the Forum with the Toronto Leafs. Defenceman Red Horner of the Leafs, then No. 1 on the Maroon Hate Parade, was handed a five-minute penalty for clobbering Hooley Smith, and took his seat beside Fergie.

From the box seats rushed a member of one of Montreal's most dignified families, Major Hartland McDougall. He waved his cane at Horner: "You should not be allowed in this league . . . you are a. . . you are. . . ."

Fergie decided a little white lie might be justified.

"Sh-h-h, major," he said, "I have just heard that Maroons have made a deal to sign Horner tomorrow."

Major McDougall stared wide-eyed at Fergie, at Horner then back to Fergie.

"Well, you've got to hand it to the boy," muttered the major, "He gives it everything he's got."

It was around that time that I saw an hilarious scene at the end of a Maroons-Canadiens sell-out game, when the fans were leaving the Forum in a state of hysteria.

The box seats then had individual chairs that were not attached to the floor. Cooper Smeaton, the referee, evoked such wrath that a prominent Montreal judge stood up in a box and threw his chair at Smeaton on the ice.

Realizing abruptly that he had left himself in a vulnerable position, the judge tugged his black homburg down over his eyes and sank into a squatting position where the chair had been. But he still stood out like a sore thumb. Smeaton signalled to nearby police, pointed at the judge in the box and barked: "Throw him out!"

The judge arose, straightened his coat, adjusted his homburg and walked down the promenade under police escort as the crowd cheered him wildly. Near the door, he recovered his full judicial dignity, turned to the vast and sympathetic crowd, and raised his homburg in salute. The survivors gave him a resounding send-off.

Years later, in 1956 at the Winter Olympics in Cortina d'Ampezzo, I saw a fan who reminded me of His Lordship. During the Canada versus Italy game, the fan took off a shoe in the open-air rink in sub-zero weather and threw it at Canada's Ken Laufman. Vigilant carabinieri swarmed around and began escorting the shoe-less fan out of the rink, limping.

The Italian goaler skated over with the shoe and the crowd forgot the Olympic spectacle to plead excitedly. The fan was allowed to recover his shoe. He put it on, shook hands with the carabinieri and left triumphantly as the fans cheered.

At a Christmas Eve game in Madison Square Garden, an outraged fan in the upper balcony became so incensed at Canadiens' Ken Reardon, who was far below on the icy reaches, that he heaved the 20-pound Christmas turkey he'd been toting home.

The turkey actually grazed Reardon, hitting the ice with a thudding impact. The startled defenceman, was reminded of a grim day not so long past when he had stood day-long, shoulder-high in the Rhine River building a bridge under incessant German bombing and shell fire.

"I've been given the bird before," Ken punned afterward, "but this one sounded like a shell from a mortar."

In Detroit during a playoff, play had to be stopped after somebody tossed a dead octopus onto the ice. Linesman George Hayes, "The Great Retriever," whirled over with a flourish to remove the obstacle and allow the game to resume. At the octopus he stopped short—to him prying battling hockey huskies apart was one thing, but picking up an octopus was another. He signalled the other linesman, who also abstained. They conferred then waved for the guys with the shovel, while some thirteen thousand of us waited for Stanley Cup history to resume its enactment.

There's a grand story about Leafs' George Armstrong in Boston. He was taking a merciless ribbing from a group of rinkside fans who were calling him all kinds of Indian—he is half Iroquois. At the end of the game Armstrong paused in front of the group.

"You guys aren't so smart," he said.

"Oh yeah?" barked one of them, "Why not?"

"I'll tell you," said the serene Armstrong, "when you white men came to this country the Indians were running things. We had no taxes. No debts. The women did all the work. How could you improve on a system like that?"

The fans were left in stitches.

In Chicago a group of historically minded fans launched a campaign to have the team name, Black Hawks, changed. They had discovered that the storied Chief Black Hawk, who left such an impression on early Chicago, had lost his biggest battle. The fan group argued that such knowledge had an adverse effect on team morale.

Gordie Howe told me of a let-down experience with a young fan.

"I had finished my third season with Detroit Red Wings," he related, "and was back in Saskatoon playing semi-pro baseball. A kid came up for my autograph. While I was signing he asked: 'Mr. Howe, what do you do in the winter'?"

Frank Selke told me of the toughest situation he ever had to face as manager-director of the Forum. This was a situation in which he said, "I tried the wisdom of Solomon and suggested that the two claimant mothers cut the baby in half. But even that didn't work."

A guy and a gal used to meet regularly in the standing room back of the uppermost seats. In time their financial situation improved to the extent that they obtained two season seats. As more time passed their friendship waned, he became engaged to another gal, she became engaged to another guy.

Each game created a crisis, as the two season-ticket holders sat unspeaking, while their betrothed partners waited out in the cold, fuming. In desperation, the two season-ticket holders finally applied for a hearing with Selke, who was so intrigued that he had them into his office and offered another pair of seats—but decidedly inferior ones.

"Would you believe it?" grins Selke, "neither would take the inferior set of seats and, as far as I know, they may be still sitting together—leaving their respective mates at home baby-sitting."

Up in the broadcasting booth at the Forum you can always find Danny Gallivan, the "voice of Canadiens." Before getting there, Danny was broadcasting hockey for a Halifax radio station. To provide fan interest, as well as allow himself "breathers," he devised a gimmick; fans were invited to send in telegrams which Danny had a young assistant read over the air.

Normally Danny would glance over the telegrams first, but one night on the road he was so exhausted that he simply waved at his raw and jittery assistant to carry on. The young fellow failed to recognize the next telegram as coming from Danny's station boss in Halifax.

"Danny Gallivan," read the assistant in tones loud and clear, "Don't give the sponsor so many plugs."

The stretch drive for the April 8, 1963 federal election came just as Leonard Patrick "Red" Kelly, Liberal member in Toronto's York West riding, entered the Stanley Cup semi-finals with his co-players in the Maple Leafs. I asked him what he intended to do.

"Hockey has given me so much for sixteen N.H.L. years," said Kelly, "that I just can't think of deserting the game and Leafs at playoff time. Even on nights between games when I'm in Toronto, I'll need to rest. Most of the voters in York West are Leaf fans, and I've told them I will let my playing make my speeches for me. They will understand."

Leafs knocked off Canadiens in five games, and Red assisted on almost one-third of the teams' goals. The York West "fans" reacted to the Kelly Campaign Sur Le Glace with a whopping total of 41,103 votes—16,661 more than his Progressive-Conservative opposition, and 2,006 more than all his three opponents combined.

But don't let all this give you the impression that fans have more fun than anybody—the owners and governors have a rousing time of it as well.

Shortly after Senator Hartland Molson took over as Canadiens' president, he had to be restrained in Chicago one night from clobbering a loud-mouth in the next box.

During the third game of the Leafs-Canadiens 1963 semifinal playoff series, C. Stafford Smythe, president of the Leafs, became so incensed over a major penalty given Eddie Shack in Montreal that he stood up in his rinkside seat, waved his coat over the glass and berated Referee Vern Buffey. Paying customers in the box seats behind complained. A Forum usherette tried in vain to have Smythe sit down. When he didn't, the usherette called two husky cops while a press cameraman lined up the scene, drooling in anticipation of

94

"shooting" the spectacle of President Smythe being hauled out right by the Leafs' bench. The cops were flexing their muscles when King Clancy ran down from an upstairs seat and pleaded the president back to normality.

The players themselves traditionally make like the zaniest of college football fans when they celebrate a Stanley Cup win. When, in 1924, Canadiens copped the venerable hardware after knocking-off Vancouver and Calgary, the celebration was an extensive affair with a late-night champagne climax in the Montreal home of Manager-Coach Leo Dandurand. Sprague Cleghorn was given the Cup to carry, and he sat with it on his knee in a closely packed Packard.

Halfway up Côte des Neiges hill, the car blew a tire. Sprague got out to help, putting the Stanley Cup down on the curb. Eventually all was well, and the celebrants continued on to Dandurand's. In the morning hours, when most of Montreal was on its way to work, somebody in the party asked: "Where's the cup?" Sprague, aghast, rushed back to Côte des Neiges hill. There was hockey's greatest prize, standing regally on the curb as it had all night. But now it was flanked by garbage cans. Not the pampered and polished symbol of today, the mug could have ended in the dump.

The late General John Reed Kilpatrick was a warm man of immense dignity while acting formally as president of New York Rangers. Yet, when exposed to the actual hockey scene, he'd revert to rabid fandom.

Some years ago, the governors of the N.H.L. decided to hold their annual mid-season meeting in Florida. They left a violent winter and gathered around a long table at West Palm Beach with the French doors at each end of the room open. The salubrious breezes so bathed the scene in utter contentment that the chairman, Conn Smythe, proposed that anybody injecting controversy into any discussion would be fined twenty-five dollars. Passed unanimously.

An hour or so passed and somebody brought up the name of Referee Red Storey. General Kilpatrick sat bolt upright:

"I think Storey is a bum," he said.

Smythe rapped his gavel. "That will cost you twenty-five dollars, General."

The General flushed and promptly held his hands wide in apology. "I'm sorry, Mr. Chairman, it was just a delayed reaction to a discussion Mr. Selke and I had about Storey before this meeting and he seemed to agree with me that...."

Smythe turned to Selke: "That will cost you twenty-five as well, Mr. Selke."

To cut a long story short, before the meeting ended Conn Smythe had to fine himself.

When the late Major Frederic McLaughlin was head of the Black Hawks, he used to berate referees from his box. During a game in which Bill Stewart (late a major baseball umpire) was refereeing, his criticism became so violent that Stewart skated over and told McLaughlin he'd have the owner thrown out of his own rink if he didn't shut up.

McLaughlin was so impressed that he hired Stewart as Black Hawks' coach—then fired him the next year.

Looking over the N.H.L. fandom in general, there is no doubt that Montreal rates as the most violent city and Chicago the nuttiest.

The Richard Riot of March 17, 1955, was tops in Montreal, of course. Provoked by President Clarence Campbell's suspension of Rocket Richard after a fracas in Boston, the fans tear-gassed the Canadiens-Detroit game to a stop at the end of the first period. Then the fire department ordered the Forum evacuated.

With the game forfeited, the unruly element in the capacity crowd took up stone-slinging in front of the rink. For four hours the rioters played havoc along St. Catherine St., breaking windows, upsetting cars, roughing up bystanders and looting jewelry shops. Thirty-seven were arrested, and the damage estimated to be $100,000. Newspapers, as far afield as the *Düsseldorf Nachrichten* in Germany, gave the riot a front-page sweepline.

In Chicago, the fans confine their havoc to the Stadium.

On April 22, 1962, when Toronto Leafs copped the Stanlev Cup there in the sixth game of the final series, the newly crowned world champions were saluted with showers of beer and ink. But that was a marked refinement, indeed, over the night of November 25, 1958, when some twenty-five explosive, plastic-covered grenades, three-quarters of an inch in diameter, were hurled from the upper balcony at the same Leafs.

President Campbell stepped in, with the result that one-hundred-dollar rewards were offered for information on the grenadiers. I got to one of them (after explaining that reporters have no need of money) and the grenadier seemed glad of the opportunity to present, anonymously, the "other side" of the matter. There was method to the mayhem.

"Twenty years ago," he explained, "we won our last Stanley Cup here. In our opinion it was the direct result of a smart guy's action down in the expensive seats—he tossed a live rabbit on the ice and jazzed everything up. Since then we've worked with eggs, heated pennies, dead fish, dead squirrels, bottles of ink and live bullets, but nothing has worked until we came up with these grenades. And wow! Our Hawks were scared not to keep skating."

Since then giant firecrackers have been introduced, supplemented by a guy with a bugle blowing "Charge!" One group actually smuggled in a six-foot-six dummy of Frank Mahovlich with a hangman's rope around its neck. They were trying to hang Big M in effigy, when the Stadium cops took away the dummy because it was a menace to the fans way down below the upper balcony.

Johnny Gottselig, former Hawk star, was fan target while doing a radio play-by-play for the Hawks' home games. When sponsorship was taken over by White Owl cigars, fans with transistor radios in the upper balcony used to wait for the commercials before lowering cords with bunches of Phillies cigars attached and dangled them in front of Gottselig.

Coach Rudy Pilous had to get himself an unlisted phone number at home, but somehow a group of fans got his number and called him up at three o'clock one morning.

"To settle an argument, Mr. Pilous," the spokesman of the group said, "can you tell me the name of the fella who has played for every team in the National Hockey League?"

"Forhellssake," growled Pilous, "why at this hour? Anyway I haven't got my record books with me in bed. . . ."

"Aw-w-w, I always said you know from nuthin' ", came the voice, "The fella is the organist in your own rink."

The caller hung up as gales of laughter sounded in the background. Pilous remained awake, raging into the dawn.

Fan enthusiasm fills rinks. It also stimulates even veteran pros. It wins hockey games—silly as it sounds, the debris-throwing nitwit does stir up things. It all adds up to why "home" ice means so much.

In the 1962 Stanley Cup final series, Leafs took a two-game lead over the Black Hawks. Shifting to the missile-mad, ear-piercing din of their Chicago Stadium, Hawks evened-up the series. After the second game, which Leafs dropped, 4-1, their Coach Imlach sighed aloud to the press: "I wish we had that kind of a crowd in Toronto; it would mean two goals to our team, just as it does to them."

The staid, almost austere, inhabitants of Maple Leaf Gardens reacted to the sentiments of Our Leader with unprecedented showers of debris in the next game at Toronto. Scandalized, the Gardens' directorate and editorial eggheads of the Toronto press combined in expressions of alarm and severe censure.

But the fans didn't really pay an attention to the spanking;

98

they were still gloating over Leafs' resounding, 8-4 come-back victory. The same Leafs were still fired up three nights later when they skated to the championship in Chicago.

The contagious, inspiring quality of N.H.L. fan enthusiasm isn't a new development—today it's only more so.

Back in 1944, when Canadiens were nearing the Stanley Cup, Tommy Gorman and Dick Irvin, both now deceased, were manager and coach respectively. After their third straight win over Hawks in the finals, Irvin locked the press out of the dressing-room but, after an interval, we heard gales of laughter inside. Eventually we learned what had happened.

Irvin had ordered the sweating Canadiens to sit down and listen. He then lashed into the players with vicious vigor, tearing a strip off the collective team's back for what he classed as a bad game. In the 3-2 win, he had seen the elements of "dangerous complacency" and was directing his most caustic comment at the top stars when the door burst open.

The effervescent Tommy Gorman had elbowed past the guard at the portal and yelled exultantly: "Wonderful game, fellows! A grand win! Terrific! Keep on like that and we'll win the Cup!"

Irvin stood appalled. Rocket Richard and Elmer Lach, seated side by side, began making choking sounds. Across the room, Toe Blake, then a line mate of the fabulous pair, hurriedly bent over his boot laces. Then, abruptly, the whole room was convulsed. Irving took a kick at a bucket, missed and joined the laughter. Only Tommy Gorman was silent—puzzledly trying to figure what he'd said that was so funny.

For better or for worse, the National Hockey League "fan fever"—even in its excesses—makes the game a living, vibrant, personal thing. The fact that the fever seeps down into dressing-rooms and up into the governors' inner sanctums is a tribute to the hell-bent all-outedness that puts hockey's Big Time into a class by itself in all the wide, wonderful, wacky world of sport.

99

CHAPTER NINE

Big Deals of the Dollar
Daredevils

*Ed Fitkin, publicity director of the Toronto Maple Leafs, faced an
unusual problem in the spring of 1948, when the team, after winning
three straight in the final playoff series, went into Detroit only one game
away from the Stanley Cup. If Leafs won, they'd have a celebration on
their hands—but where? Detroit was jammed with conventions involved
in peacetime change-overs, and American money was on limited supply.*

*He spoke to Manager Conn Smythe who finally suggested trying to
book the Penobscot Club on an "if" basis. The owner somewhat
reluctantly agreed but stressed that he be given a fair warning.*

*With ten minutes to go in the game, and Leafs leading, 7-2, Fitkin
whispered to Smythe: "Should I phone the Penobscot Club now?"*

*"Get away from me!" roared Smythe, "What are you trying to do—
jinx us?"*

In early 1963 the Toronto Stock Exchange issued a pamphlet
that left its limited readership bug-eyed. It drew attention to
the fact that if a fellow had purchased one thousand Maple
Leaf Gardens' shares at one dollar a share, when first listed
in 1935, and hadn't disturbed the dividends through the years,
he'd have a bundle of some $190,000 at the current market
rate of $32.00 per share.

At the end of the regular 1962/63 season, President Campbell
left promoters throughout the sport world talking to themselves over his disclosure that the six teams had set an attend-
ance record "close to the saturation point" for the 210 league

games. Over that long route the crowds averaged 13,008 a game, 92 per cent of the rated seated capacity. The playoffs, of course, averaged 100 per cent.

Put the two items together and you may assume without fear of contradiction that the owners are reaping in the lovely green stuff. There is reason to believe that, if it keeps up, the annual meetings of the governors will have to be held at Fort Knox.

But research into N.H.L. history tells you it wasn't always so; you'll find another type of hockey hero, largely unsung, who never had to worry about shedding blood—but sweat and tears they shed. They were the Dollar Daredevils of yesteryear.

Their risks were not the physical ones faced on the ice by mighty men in mighty moments, but they did risk fortunes. With each team that folded after entering the N.H.L., a fortune went down the drain. A cold, realistic business approach would never have kept these Dollar Daredevils in there fighting through the grim depression years. There had to be something deeper, something intermingling love of the game with confidence in its future.

Two cities, Montreal and Toronto, have to be regarded as the rock foundation upon which the N.H.L. of today was built. In these great cities the Dollar Daredevils scorned the bitterest blasts of the depression winter by not being content with mere survival. During the depression that was blowing down numberless edifices of industry, they dared build monuments to Big Time hockey in the Forum and Maple Leaf Gardens respectively.

The importance of the two monuments has never been fully appreciated. It was 1924, and major hockey in the West was folding despite new arenas and new ideas, when Senator Donat Raymond of Montreal dared organize the building in Montreal of the first rink primarily designed for hockey. Ignoring the head-shaking in financial circles, and investing heavily from his own funds, he formed the Canadian Arena Company. He insisted on the first departure from the old skating-rink design in order to ensure clear view for all spectators.

In 1929, amid the crumbling chaos of The Crash, the most daring of all the Dollar Daredevils, Conn Smythe, began his incredible campaign that led to Maple Leaf Gardens.

If these two cities had faltered, if they had been content with just surviving in leaky-roof operations, if they hadn't shown such inspirational confidence in the game's future at that crucial time, I can't imagine the American cities risking vast fortunes in continuing support of a new game comparatively unknown to the vast majority of American adult fans and unplayed by their children.

With all due deference to the gamble made by the American cities, the daring of Montreal and Toronto can only be classed as being of heroic dimensions.

Boston, New York, Detroit and Chicago—to name today's American entries as examples—had already established arenas in which to operate. And money was no major problem with them.

Boston came in with the backing of Charles F. Adams, who headed sport interests that included major baseball's Boston Braves. When the Pacific Coast League folded the year after, Adams calmly offered $200,000 for all the players in the league.

New York's Tex Rickard, of course, was backed by greenbacks unlimited at Madison Square. The Detroit entry was shaky but not for long—in came James D. Norris, a hockey enthusiast who had started a vast fortune from grain dealing in the Canadian West. Chicago began with a quarter of a million dollars—provided by socialite and polo player Major Frederic McLaughlin, plus a group of sporty friends "serving without profit for the good of the game." One of their first

102

ventures was to spend $150,000 of the money in buying the Portland Rosebuds. Among their starting stars were such men as Dick Irvin, Cully Wilson, Rabbit McVeigh, famed goalie Hugh Lehman and Babe Dye. They added eastern stars as well.

Again, the American teams were fortunate in having available for hiring an unusually formidable array of established Canadian hockey personalities to direct the ice operation. Boston got Art Ross, New York got Lester Patrick, Detroit got Art Duncan and Chicago got Pete Muldoon. These veterans of the major hockey battlefield had, by and large, ready-made armies supplied them by the folding of the Pacific loop, while the eagerness of amateur prospects across Canada to join the American surge removed immediate need for farm-team development.

Just how facile the building of these new franchises was can be evidenced by Rangers' winning the Stanley Cup in the team's second year of existence. Boston made it to the Cup finals in the third season and won it in the fourth. Chicago reached the finals in the fifth season, won it in the eighth. Detroit made it to the finals in eight seasons, won the Cup in ten.

In all of these American cities the risks were purely part of multi-million-dollar sport operations. If hockey had failed in New York, for example, the venture would simply have been written off without affecting the overall Madison Square operation. Failure in Pittsburgh and Philadelphia was just dollar less, not disaster. Business kept on as usual.

But, in Montreal and Toronto, the gambles were made at massive risk, when financial backers were few and extremely leery and the fans short of spending money. The daring of the Dollar Daredevils in raising the huge monuments designed primarily for hockey had to be appraised at the time as nothing short of foolhardy.

When reading about 92 per cent of all N.H.L. seats sold over the 1962/63, 210-game schedule, I found myself contrasting the scene with that I recall after seeing my first N.H.L. game.

I was in high school in Montreal, and Canadiens, then playing at the barn-like Mount Royal Arena, used to send down batches of complimentary seats to fill the big, empty gaps. My first "comp" left me watching Howie Morenz, Aurel Joliat and the immortal goalie Georges Vezina—for free!

Only a few years previously, Canadiens had been purchased (in 1921) for $11,000 by three Montreal sportsmen, Joe Cattarinich, Louis Letourneau and Leo Dandurand. They were thought to have acted on the reckless side, in view of the feeble fan following. Incidentally, they bought the team from the widow of the late George Kennedy who had paid $7,500 for the club.

In 1935, the owners, now down to two—Cattarinich, sixty per cent; Dandurand, forty per cent—sold out to Senator Raymond, as head of the Canadian Arena Company, for $165,000.

Once again, the Senator drew critical comment in financial circles. It looked to all but him that good money was being sent after bad.

The Forum, built in 1924 for $1,250,000, had felt the full force of the depression storm. The Montreal Maroons made their debut with the opening of the new rink and won the Stanley Cup the next season—the same season that saw Canadiens move into the Forum.

Two N.H.L. teams in such times were just too much for Montreal fans' wallets. I recall selling programmes at games which drew only nine hundred. A $250,000 mortgage held by the Sun Life provoked a crisis, but it was met.

The Maroons won the Stanley Cup again in 1935, but lost money in so doing. That's where Senator Raymond's stubborn confidence in the game prompted another daring gamble;

104

he saw in Canadiens' fire-wagon style of hockey a crowd-pleasing element that would not only survive but grow in appeal. He bought the Canadiens. Maroons folded three years later, but the Canadiens' star remained on the rise.

Fortune favours the brave; when for reasons of health he had to retire in 1957, Senator Raymond sold controlling interest in the Canadian Arena Company (embracing the Forum and the Canadiens' organization) for a reported two million dollars. The total value of the company's holdings was estimated at $4,500,000.

The purchaser, Senator Hartland Molson, representing the Molson brewing family, took a lot of kidding around Montreal. A former Battle of Britain fighter pilot, and highly popular in local sport circles, the story circulated that he had grown fed up trying to get seats at the Forum which had then been sold-out for seven years. So he bought the place and made himself president of Canadiens. This got him into the dressing-room—even without knocking.

In all fairness, Hartland was undoubtedly a daring young man in a Spitfire. He once got himself shot up at 24,000 feet, bailed out and pulled the parachute cord only at 7,000 feet because the Germans were shooting down chutes at the time. But he could hardly be classed as a Dollar Daredevil. The Molsons had quite a few millions lying around loose, and the purchase was a gilt-edged investment—the Forum has now been sold out for over thirteen years. But there was a nostalgic touch with yesteryear; Senator Hartland Molson's late father, Colonel Herbert Molson, had been a director of the Maroons when they had opened the Forum in 1924.

Hartland's first policy meeting with Managing Director Frank Selke was a dramatic tribute to major hockey—he told Selke to consider dividends secondary to keeping Canadiens as "worthy representatives of Quebec province." He stressed that the purchase was strictly a family affair and not to be

105

construed as an advertising medium for the Molson brewing industry.

But the dollar's importance couldn't be treated so casually thirty-two years before—when, in 1925, the hockey debacle in the west called for dollar daring in the east.

Back in 1910, the famed Patrick brothers, Frank and Lester had tasted the Renfrew (Ontario) Millionaires' riches in the National Hockey Association and returned home to Nelson, British Columbia, with a bright dream aborning. They persuaded their father, a prosperous lumberman, to sell his vast interests and invest in the establishment of a rival major league in the west, the Pacific Coast League. They built artificial rinks (first of their kind in North America) in Victoria and Vancouver. Frank introduced new rules to jazz up the game, rules that became national. They raided eastern teams for players, and the league boomed for five years.

Originally the league in which Frank was president comprised Vancouver, New Westminster and Victoria. Exigencies later caused the transfer of franchises, so that at one time or another Seattle, Portland, Spokane and Tacoma had teams operating, though the league was never larger than a four-team affair.

It might still be booming if World War I hadn't cut into the revenues. Fan support dropped off, although the western teams won the Stanley Cup in 1915 (Vancouver), in 1917 (Seattle) and in 1925 (Victoria). Word got around that the Patricks were ready to sell out.

When Boston's Adams offered $200,000 for the entire playing personnel of the western loop, Frank Patrick officially accepted. But such a storm blew up among other N.H.L. clubs that Adams reluctantly agreed to spread his blessings—although insisting that Bruins get several big names, Eddie Shore above all. It worked out well for the Patricks who, after the new wave of negotiations ended, made $300,000 instead of $200,000.

But no Dollar Daredevil story comes close to matching that of the incomparable Conn Smythe. They say Conn came into the world yelling and never stopped. There must be some truth to the claim, because today, years after he relinquished the Leafs' presidency to his son Stafford, the echoes of his yells can still be distinctly heard as you wander backstage through the dust-free, always freshly painted corridors of the finest hockey palace ever built, the Maple Leaf Gardens.

In Frank Selke's book *Behind the Cheering*, one of the many wonderful stories about the master of the Smythsonian Institute (as egghead sportwriters in Toronto re-christened the Gardens) struck me as being the first evidence of the reckless daring mixed with keen hockey savvy that eventually made Conn the dominant personality of the National Hockey League.

At the age of nineteen, he had won a name for himself as captain of the Toronto Varsity Juniors. At twenty, with World War I underway, he became a junior officer in the newly organized 40th Battery that sparkled with famous sport names. To boost recruiting for overseas, the Battery entered a hockey team in the senior series of the Ontario Hockey Association. Conn was made manager and assembled a squad that was understandably not up to the calibre of their long-established rival clubs. But Conn and his soldiers oozed spirit that promptly won them an enthusiastic following in war-excited Toronto.

The fourth game was against the formidable Toronto Argonauts, rated a "sure thing" over the Battery boys.

The night before the game Conn got in on a secret—the Battery would be leaving for overseas almost immediately afterwards. Just how Conn did it nobody knows to this day, but he got his hands on the entire officers' mess fund, which had piled up to an impressive $7,000 in preparation for farewell parties and other expenses associated with the big-shift overseas.

Strange things began to happen. For one, a rumour spread

107

around Toronto sporting circles that a certain gambler of dubious reputation was giving big odds on the Argonauts. Lesser gamblers, now surer than ever of a sure thing, promptly upped the odds of anybody wishing to bet against the Argonauts. Conn got every dollar of the mess fund covered—at the highest odds.

Down through the years I've heard various versions of Conn's pre-game pep talk to the Battery team. But all agree it was the most dynamite-packed pep talk in the history of hockey. It was also the briefest oration ever delivered by Smythe. He told them in simple terms that the overseas adventure was so close that this would be their last game— possibly the last time many of them would ever be on skates. He added that every last dime of the mess fund was riding on them.

The Battery boys didn't even bother opening the dressing-room door; they crashed through the damn thing. In the first eight minutes of play, they piled up a 5-0 lead, and the Argonauts never did recover from the shock. In terms of festive fixings, the 40th Battery was probably the best-equipped Canadian unit that went overseas in World War I.

After the war, when New York Rangers entered the scene, Conn had an extremely short session as manager and coach. When he found he couldn't be boss, he blew a fuse, turned over the reins to Lester Patrick and returned to his beloved Toronto —and enthusiastic supporting of the St. Pats team which had changed its name to Maple Leafs.

The team ended 1926/27 with a forty-thousand dollar deficit, and Conn was put in charge. He immediately decided to place his hopes on a crop of young players (including Charlie Conacher, Joe Primeau, Red Horner and Busher Jackson) who had been brought along as Marlboro Juniors by Coach Frank Selke.

This policy switch to youth allowed Conn to peddle off

established N.H.L. players. The Leafs' directors were startled, but their worries were eased somewhat by finding the deficit wiped out and replaced by a $70,000 bank account. What's more, the popular young stars were drawing crowds to the old Mutual Street Arena.

But Smythe wasn't happy. He told the world that if Leafs wanted to stay in the N.H.L. and compete on an equal basis with the opulent American teams and the richly backed Montreal Maroons, a bigger and better rink than the Mutual Street Arena was needed. Nobody took Conn's comments seriously then, and as the depression's full force hit during the 1929/30 winter, he was thought to have gone completely crackers. That man was yelling for a new $1,500,000 arena!

The first major publicity medium Conn's persuasive sales talk captivated was Greg Clark, then top columnist of the *Toronto Star* and now Associate Editor of *Weekend Magazine*. Conn then got Foster Hewitt pumping for the scheme on the hockey broadcasts, and he followed up by having Frank Selke put out a special programme containing preliminary drawings of "the new arena."

It made nice listening and reading, but it would probably have remained "dream stuff" if it wasn't for a race horse named Rare Jewel.

Rare Jewel, owned by Conn Smythe, was a filly with a chronic affection for the lonely end of the track. In the early summer of 1930, the nag ended last five times, and second to last in a sixth race. This was the record she toted into the Coronation Stakes at Woodbine, for which she had been nominated before birth. Racing insiders kidded Conn mercilessly—some said there was danger that Rare Jewel would get lapped by the favourite, Seagram's great Spherette.

But Conn had been rising extra early in the mornings to stand with watch in hand as Rare Jewel worked out. Nobody else bothered to clock the filly. What the watch told the amazed Smythe prompted him to bet $60—$20 on win, $20 on place and $20 on show.

Rare Jewel paid $219 to win, $49 to place and $18 to show. Besides the $4,000 purse, Conn gathered in some $10,000 from mutuel and other wagers. Calling in Frank Selke, now his right hand in hockey, Conn shoved the heap of money across his desk and said: "The Ottawa Senators are feeling the financial strain; I hear they will listen to an offer for King Clancy."

Rare Jewel's green harvest (plus a couple of players) went as down-payment on a $35,000 deal that brought Clancy to the Leafs, and a new hockey excitement was born in Toronto. The over-crowding of the old arena suddenly made Conn's yelling for a new arena take on a semblance of sense.

A long list of prominent names came into the incredible financing adventure that followed. Conn used everybody. Bigwigs were deked into buying stock by fictional stories about other bigwigs being interested. Eaton's vigorously opposed the idea of a sporting arena so close to their posh College Street store, and they ended by giving an option on the land where the Gardens now stand as well as buying $25,000 in stock.

When a board of directors' meeting concluded, there wasn't enough stock sold to warrant going ahead on the actual construction. Frank Selke, an electrician by trade and a union executive, went before executives of the Allied Building Trades Council with a proposal. He asked skilled workers to agree to take twenty per cent of their pay in stock certificates. "Otherwise many will stay unemployed." He argued there, and at every meeting he could find, by telling them he was so sure of the Gardens' future that he had raised $3,500 by mortgaging his home for stock.

The contractors were so impressed by labour's gesture, that they invested in heavy-stock purchases. The bank involved was so impressed by labour and contractors that it bought $25,000 in preferred stock.

On went the green light. Five months later, Conn Smythe's dream came true, as the Maple Leafs skated out to play their first game in the spanking new Gardens. The date was November 12, 1931. He had out-snarled the depression.

As for Selke, he had managed to raise another thousand dollars for stock, making an investment of $4,500. In 1946, when he split with Conn Smythe and moved to Montreal as boss man of Canadiens, Selke sold his holdings for $34,000. Some of the skilled workers who reluctantly took stock certificates in lieu of full pay in 1931, now have their dividend cheques sent to them in Florida during our harsh Canadian winters.

After winning his spurs in a modest way as a Dollar Daredevil in Toronto, Selke flashed this flare in a major way in 1956. But, surprisingly, few people know about it today.

Selke had heard murmurs to the effect that Detroit's all-star left winger, Ted Lindsay, 163 pounds of meanness and greatness, was no longer on speaking terms with Jack Adams, then general manager of the Red Wings. Lindsay was, in 1956, also a candidate for No. 1 spot on the Hate Parade in the Montreal Forum, but Selke knew how closely akin can be hate and love with hockey fans. Those fans had never expected to see Rocket Richard still zooming for Canadiens, when his kid brother Henri would make the grade. Yet there were the two brothers, both major stars, playing together—Henri at centre, Rocket on right wing.

And now Selke's imagination visualized a sight for the gods—the two Richards with Ted Lindsay on left wing. For sheer surge and skill, the line had a potential position up with the most fabulous lines of all time.

Selke offered Adams $100,000 "just for Lindsay's contract." On top of that, of course, there would be the not-so-little matter of the Canadien salary for Lindsay.

Adams, however, wanted no part of strengthening the

111

already powerful Canadiens, who were riding a five-year reign as Stanley Cup champs; instead, he traded away Turbulent Ted to the Chicago Black Hawks, who had been in the N.H.L. cellar for four years.

Of course, Selke had good reason to believe there was magic in the nice round figure he offered. Three years before it had worked in a sensational fashion for the most trying experience he ever had with signing a player.

Jean Beliveau, pride and joy of Quebec City, had made a shambles of junior hockey. In 1950/51 he came up to Canadiens for two games, had a goal and an assist. But he shrugged off Canadiens' offers—the story was that he was doing better as an "amateur" junior in Quebec City than the top N.H.L. star. His next two seasons in the Quebec Senior Hockey League were spent in the headlines. In 150 regular and playoff games, he whipped in 123 goals and assisted on 102 others. During the second season he took time off for a three-game stint with Canadiens and scored five goals in the three games.

The fan pressure grew so intense that Selke finally called in Beliveau and signed him to a five-year contract. Afterwards I asked Selke just how he had managed to do it.

"It was really quite simple," said Selke, "all I did was open the Forum safe and say, 'Help yourself, son.' "

The exact amount was never officially disclosed because of possible repercussions among the established Canadien star cast, but I have it on "inside" authority that the contract called for $100,000 for the five seasons plus bonuses. It paid off: with his help, Canadiens won five consecutive Stanley Cups. However, the shrugging off of Selke's $100,000 offer to Detroit for Lindsay's contract indicated to me that the Dollar Daredevil had been washed away by the wave of prosperity hitting hockey. And I felt that way for six years—until the night of October 5, 1962.

The annual All-Star Game is preceded, the evening before, by a festive All-Star Dinner tossed by the N.H.L. All club officials get along well together at this affair because nobody has lost or even tied a game as yet. The October 5th spread at the Royal York Hotel followed tradition and was even more spirited than ever.

Eyewitnesses at the post-dinner party have proven a little unreliable, but the principals in The Story that dwarfed the All-Star Game itself were Chicago owner Jim Norris and Toronto industrialist Hal Ballard, executive vice-president of the Leafs.

Apparently the episode started with Jim expansively rating Leaf star Frank Mahovlich as one of the greatest ever, adding: "I'd give a million dollars for him."

The story goes that Ballard smiled: "You're kidding, Jim."

Now, Big Jim doesn't kid about any one of those little, sixty millions of dollars he reportedly kept tucked away for a rainy day. He allegedly reacted to the "kidding" comment by pulling out his spending money, peeling off $1,000, handing it to the astonished Ballard as "down payment" and shook hands "to seal the bargain."

In all fairness it should be recognized that Ballard alone hadn't enough authority to make such a deal and treated the episode as party hi-jinks to be resolved with laughs on the morrow. But the morning found Chicago general manager Tommy Ivan at the Maple Leaf Gardens with a Norris-signed cheque for one million dollars in Canadian funds. Scott Young of the *Globe and Mail* thought it was penny-pinching on Norris' part since Canadian funds would save him $80,000 in exchange.

"Do I take Mahovlich home with me," asked Ivan, "or do you deliver?"

The uproar stirred by press, radio and television over the weekend resulted in the calling of a special meeting on Monday morning. Outside the Gardens, protesting fans formed a picket line carrying signs such as "Don't Sell Mahovlich" and the switchboard received "we'll burn you down" threats. At the meeting were president Stafford Smythe, vice-president Ballard and publisher John Bassett, currently the top money men behind the Gardens.

The meeting admitted to having been tempted by "the fantastic offer," but they decided to turn it down for the good of team and hockey in Toronto. In Chicago, Norris asked: "What offer? It was a deal and the Leafs welched." When he calmed down, Jim issued a terse official announcement that he considered the matter closed, adding: "Evidently the Toronto club regard Mahovlich as highly as I did."

Absent from the meeting had been the chairman of the board, Conn Smythe, who heard the decision with mixed feelings—which was understandable. Forty years before, when fighting frantically to build the Gardens, Conn would cheerfully have given both legs and at least one arm for a million bucks.

President Clarence Campbell commented: "I believe it was a serious offer, even if it was uneconomical." However, I got the impression he was tickled pink about the affair. The story made headlines across the major baseball front in World Series time. The name of Norris takes the episode out of the "publicity gag" status and leaves the baseball fraternity suddenly looking in awed respect upon the N.H.L. Only players Willie Mays and Herb Score had ever been mentioned in the million-dollar category of major ball.

As for Campbell, he undoubtedly deserves a rating somewhere in the ranks of the Dollar Daredevils, although he hasn't a dollar invested in the N.H.L.

Frank Calder, a former sports writer, had been secretary of the old National Hockey Association before the N.H.L. came into being in 1917. As president of the new league, he guided the operation fairly and fearlessly through stormy seas—from one war and into another, with a depression in between. After twenty-six strenuous years at the helm, he died quietly on February 4th, 1943, with a portfolio of N.H.L. business papers spread on his bed.

Mervyn "Red" Dutton, former playing star and N.H.L. coach, was persuaded to take over. Dutton, a battle-scarred veteran of World War I, and deeply hit by the loss of two sons in World War II, made it clear that he accepted the post purely as a "pinch-hitter" to help out the game that had helped establish him as a major western contractor.

In 1961 I went out to watch the handsome redhead ride his frisky horse as president of the Calgary Stampede and was told that he was well up in the multi-million dollar bracket after building airports in the very-far north and running oil lines clean across the Rockies.

One of Dutton's outstanding skills lay in selecting and obtaining top-drawer executive aides. He set as target an Edmonton lawyer and Rhodes Scholar who, before enlisting, had impressed the N.H.L. as the referee of one hundred and fifty-five regular and twelve playoff games. In 1945, Lieutenant-Colonel Campbell was acting as prosecutor at the War Trials in Germany and, like all veterans, doing some pondering about his rehabilitation problem, when a cable arrived from Dutton. It asked if he, Campbell, would be interested in a job as assistant to the president?

Campbell cabled back promptly and affirmatively. When he heard no more from Dutton, he thought the whole deal was off. But on returning to Canada he dropped into National Hockey League headquarters in Montreal. Dutton gave him a big welcome and closed the office door. When it opened Dutton announced that the rather dazed Campbell was the new N.H.L. president.

Life as prexy of the vast hockey empire hasn't been easy, but Campbell has weathered the storms well. His suspension of Rocket Richard in 1955 brought threats on his life as well as threats to dynamite the Sun Life Building in which the N.H.L. headquarters are located. At the Forum he was showered with eggs and fruit and physically assaulted. Critical press ink, showered on him through the years, would suffice to float a light cruiser. He was blamed (and didn't deny blame) over the protest resignation of Referee "Red" Storey. He was in the middle of the 1963 libel-suit resignation of Referee Eddie Powers. Of his six bosses—the governors of the N.H.L.—there is nearly always at least one bitterly critical, but Campbell takes it all in stride: "It's inevitable in this controversial business." As for owners who rage at him, he is sympathetic: "I bear in mind that to be a good owner you must have one foot on the bench."

Campbell's contract as president and secretary-treasurer of the N.H.L. is unique in sport. It simply goes on and on from year to year; it calls for no re-negotiation. It can be terminated by either the governors or Campbell with two years' notice. If he feels his salary (said to be $25,000 or more) needs adjusting, he simply makes a proposal to the governors.

The N.H.L. itself is an anomaly. Its name is not even registered. It is a partnership of corporations, all independent, operating under terms of a contract among them. There is only one "signing" executive officer, Campbell. The governors give him a set of by-laws with very specific powers, including absolute power in the touchy matter of enforcing discipline.

While President Campbell can't take credit for the post-war boom in the national economy, he must receive considerable credit as the administrator of a Big Business whose gate receipts have increased sixty per cent since he took over.

During that period the wealth has been liberally shared with the players, whose gross income has more than doubled. Today's players earn an average of $17,000 annually, including bonuses and incentive money.

The average salary, exclusive of "extras," is more than $13,000. The added incentive money—one of Campbell's pet plans for continued stimulation of the game—now hits a whopping total of $220,000. This figure includes $135,000 awarded players of the four teams making the playoffs, as well as the All-Star bonus money upped in 1962/63 from $9,000

Photo La Presse by Roger St Jean

Canada Wide Photos

Hockey's ugliest moment: during Richard Riot of 1955, egg-bespattered N.H.L. President Clarence Campbell is attacked by black-jacketed hoodlum.

The morning after sees the windows of the Montreal Forum shattered. Jewellery store at bottom was one of store victims on St. Catherine St. in $100,000 looting.

David Bier Studios

Alexandra Studio

Coach Dick Irvin gave prophetic "V for Victory" as manager Frank Selke beamed at Jean Beliveau's signing in 1955 (reportedly $100,000 for five years). Jean helped Canadiens to five consecutive Stanley Cups. At right, Conn Smythe photoed in fine voice.

Leafs' Frank Mahovlich (27) scores against Chicago at Toronto.

to $18,000. Bonus money allocated for the trophy awards was doubled to $6,500.

The added incentive scheme has paid off dramatically; even with Rangers and Boston "out" of playoff contention, with over a month to go in 1962/63, they remained fighting like demons for All-Star and trophy bonuses. This incentive intrigued me when noted in the case of three-man lines where only one player was in contention for an award, yet his mates battled as if for themselves.

Campbell personally supervised the monumental two-year task of establishing the Pensions Society which has resulted in a happier future for the players and other league personnel. The fund has now accumulated some three million dollars, but Campbell had trouble putting it across; many players resented paying nine hundred dollars a year even for future security. Campbell produced a "sales pitch" that won the day.

"You can save $900 a year painlessly," he told the players, "by driving a car with a six-inch shorter wheelbase." Campbell had auto experts figure it out for him.

So the N.H.L. is now Big Business solidly established. With all-time record attendances, there seem to be only golden sunrises ahead without a cloud on the horizon. But I suppose the movie industry felt that way too—once upon a time.

There has been much talk of expansion to such west-coast points as Los Angeles and San Francisco where hockey has blossomed of late. But N.H.L. owners are leery; they point out that baseball expansion clicked there immediately because ready-made teams—Brooklyn Dodgers to Los Angeles and New York Giants to San Francisco—eliminated the strenuous and perilous building stage for fan backing. The owners feel that expanding with either western or eastern newcomer teams would only tend to weaken the formidably successful N.H.L. structure.

There is, in my opinion, one interesting expansion challenge worthy of the Dollar Daredevil tradition in hockey's Big Time.

As a veteran press-box observer for more than thirty years, I dare feel my suggestion is worthy of a bit of consideration. Maturity allows that privilege, while the experience of the movie industry indicates today's hockey boom carries no assurance of continuation tomorrow. My suggestion was really born in England while I was there in early 1963.

I had never been quite clear about how the highly complex major-league soccer operation functions, so I took a few days to study its operation with executives and press people explaining.

Briefly: whereas the N.H.L. is a six-team operation, the Football League (major soccer equivalent) has ninety-two teams divided into four divisions of decreasing calibre.

The First Division has the cream of the big-money, crowd-pulling teams of England and Wales, and the team finishing first is champ.

The two teams finishing at the bottom of First Division are are "relegated" or demoted to the Second Division at the end of each season, while the two top teams of Second Division are promoted. In Third Division, the bottom four teams are relegated, while the top four of the Fourth Division are promoted. It's rough going at the bottom of the Fourth Division; the last four teams must apply for re-election (which is not automatic) or drop out. Meanwhile, improving teams from other leagues are always posting applications to replace the lowest teams on the soccer totem pole.

The Football Association, a parliament of soccer governing the game from schools to major pro level, runs a separate competition for the game's most dramatic trophy, the F.A. Cup. It's a trophy that any team in England or Wales may challenge. The association divides the challenges into categories, and survivors move on. In terms of hockey, it could end up with Toronto Maple Leafs facing an amateur team from Moosomin, Saskatchewan, for The Cup.

From all this comes my suggestion for expansion: it's

generally agreed that the four top pro leagues in North America rate this way: (1) N.H.L., (2) American League, (3) Western League and (4) Eastern Pro League. Couldn't the whole shebang be pulled into one major league of four divisions, with relegation for the bottom team and promotion for the top team? The bottom spot in the Fourth Division would be the door through which new-blood teams could enter.

The team finishing atop the head would get the recognition it doesn't get now—the result of a seventy-game schedule becomes secondary to the post-season playoffs for the Stanley Cup. This would give the stately Prince of Wales Trophy (ever hear of it?) the prestige it deserves. Today it goes to the scheduled season champion team, but it lives in the shadow of Lord Stanley's hardware.

As for the Stanley Cup itself, let it revert to the role its donor intended back in 1893—that of a challenge trophy. Let it become the F.A. Cup of hockey, with an even wider aspect. Let it be open to world-wide hockey. Cup games could be run off simultaneously with the four-division pro league games. And it could boil down to the two finalists being Maple Leafs versus Russia. Wouldn't you go if you could snaffle ducats? What would television pay for that one—in North America and via satellite beaming overseas?

I can see several immediate benefits: (1) New hockey interest would be stimulated all down the line without affecting the calibre of any division. For instance, if the end of 1962/63 saw Boston relegated, and the top American League team promoted, it could be a fairly even swap. The threat of relegation might have fired the Boston team to new peaks in the last month, while the A.L. fight at the top for promotion would have fired that league, too. And 1963/64 would have N.H.L. fans watching a new team, while the A.L. cities would be stimulated by seeing a whole new array of major teams they had hitherto only read about. As for Boston fans, they might be better off—if the N.H.L. is really that much superior they'd

119

be rooting in 1963/64 for a league-leading A.L. team instead of a tail-ender N.H.L. team.

(2) It would stimulate players right down to grass-roots hockey. The ladder would be now open for climbing instead of a rather vague waiting for breaks. A team fighting its way from fourth division to midway in the second would command serious consideration of its playing personnel by First Division clubs whose scouts had hitherto seen them playing only against lower-level competition.

(3) The Cup games would give hockey executives and fans alike a complete new look at a vast array of talent they now have no way of really judging. Overseas hockey has possibly gone as far as it can go; it needs major competition to improve. And don't tell me teams like Boston and Rangers couldn't do with a new field of talent.

Maybe this plan would decrease the revenue of today's N.H.L. clubs. But maybe, given ingenious direction, it wouldn't. For instance, new talent would be cheaper and other sources of revenue (such as international and transatlantic television) could make up. And a rich compensation bonus, I honestly feel, would come in, effectively warding off any potential wane of interest, such as fell so suddenly upon a booming Hollywood.

The men of hockey stay young, and Norris' million-dollar cheque convinced me the Dollar Daredevil spirit still lives. But the complacency of success is insidious; it creeps in gradually and causes folks to stop looking at exciting new horizons.

As I wrap up this all-too-incomplete history of Headline Hockey, there comes to mind the words of Bernard Baruch, who rose from poverty to a multi-millionaire Wall Street Tycoon in his early thirties and became trusted counsellor to seven United States presidents: "It is not so important where you came from as where you are going."

EPILOGUE

The veteran French-Canadian elevator operator taking me up to the newspaper office on the morning of April 8, 1963, ignored my "Good Morning!" to unburden his soul with: "I never thought I'd say it, but Bobby Hull is greater than was Howie Morenz."

The previous night he had been watching television as Hull and his team, Chicago Black Hawks, were knocked out of the playoff semi-finals by the Red Wings in Detroit, 7-4. Hull, close-checked to the point of handcuffing, had literally erupted with one of the most spectacular displays of Stanley Cup history. Even under a seven-goal barrage, he refused to acknowledge defeat and figured in all four Hawk goals, scoring three and assisting on the other.

But what made this eruption truly something for hockey memories was that this magnificent exhibition of fighting hockey came from a man who had no right to be out of hospital. In a previous playoff game he had suffered a nose fracture that club president Jim Norris, once ruler of the boxing world, said was "worse than anything I ever saw come out of a ring." The nose was mashed right up to where it joined the skull. Yet Hull, ignoring medical pleas, had left Chicago and caught a plane on his own decision to join his team in Detroit.

He played partially blinded by an eyeball turned scarlet and a nose cast that hindered view from the other eye. In addition, a severe shoulder injury, from the latter part of the regular season, cut down the force of his shooting. But consummate courage and skill, plus the challenge of championship, had produced enough goals to win any normal playoff game—even the overpowering Red Wings had been unable to contain this one Hawk.

As I walked from the elevator, the operator's comment on Morenz stayed with me—the Morenz who had died two years before Hull was born.

At my desk the mail remained unopened as my recollection of another conversational link with Morenz returned. Two years previously, I was sitting in the home of Canadiens' Bernie "Boom Boom" Geoffrion. Beside him on the divan was his wife, Marlene, daughter of the late Howie. Playing in front of them were their two perpetual-motion boys, supremely oblivious of the drama in the two big photos hanging side-by-side on the wall above. One was of their father, taken after the Boomer had won the N.H.L. scoring title the year before—passing Howie's lifetime total of 270 goals. The other photo was of the boys' grandfather, Howie.

The scene had me day-dreaming until a quiet query from the Boomer startled me into wide-awakedness.

"Tell us, Andy," he asked, "just how good was Howie?"

I looked from him to Marlene, both gazing intently and realized neither had ever seen the fabulous Howie play.

In that setting, it was the most difficult question I had ever faced. I don't recall all of my stumbling reply, but I did stress that Howie—and his later-generation successor the Canadien super-star Rocket Richard—had one thing in common. Neither ever recognized defeat. On bad nights when Canadiens had been buried under an avalanche of goals and the wait-until-next-game mentality had taken over, I have seen both Howie and Rocket take on whole N.H.L. teams single-handed. And, often, I've seen their surge light a fire that lifted Canadiens into a hellbent-for-goals attack to leave vast and hostile crowds limping from the violence of desire steaming up from the ice.

Just as Bobby Hull had done on the night of April 7, 1963.

I feel it's unfair, if not downright impossible, to compare the builders and players of yesteryear with those of today.

Big Time hockey is akin to a towering and still-growing edifice. As we stand back to admire it, there is a natural temptation to eulogize the glamorous guys who work today on the high steel. But are they any more worthy of eulogy than the toilers of yesteryear who laid the sturdy foundation upon which the great edifice has risen?

Actually, if you could look down upon a game in which both Howie Morenz and Bobby Hull were going all-out, the only difference you'd likely find would be in the colour of their sweaters.

POSTSCRIPT

If you ever get close enough to the Stanley Cup to read the names engraved on it, pause, friend. Adjust the back lighting or the position of your head so you can squint through the sheen and reflection on its highly polished surface. You'll find recorded there the rosters of teams that have literally contributed sweat, blood and tears to their winning since the National Hockey League's inception in 1917. It has never been won the easy way.

Peer with me and day-dream as I have often done of stirring sagas of hockeydom. Perhaps you too will find yourself plucking players from the greatest teams of the past and forming a "dream team" all your own. Listen closely as imagination sees that wondrous array in action, and certainly you will hear the tumult and the shouting.

If as you walk away, friend, a pang of sadness is felt on realizing your team can never be, that so many of your greats cannot skate from yesteryear, grieve not. In memory's eye there is no end to the Immortal League in which they now play, and no limit to the hockey peaks they can still climb.   ANDY O'BRIEN

1917/18   TORONTO ARENAS—Rusty Crawford, Harry Meeking, Ken Randall, Corb Dennenny, Harry Cameron, Jack Adams, Alf Skinner, Harry Mummery, Happy Holmes, Reg Noble, Charlie Querrie (*manager*), Dick Carroll (*coach*), Frank Carroll (*trainer*).

1918/19   NO DECISION—Series halted by Spanish influenza epidemic, illness of several players and death of Joe Hall of the Canadiens from flu. Five games had been played when the series was halted, each team having won two and tied one.

1919/20   OTTAWA SENATORS—Jack McKell, Jack Darragh, Morley Bruce, Horace Merrill, George (Buck) Boucher, Eddie Gerard, Clint Benedict, Sprague Cleghorn, Frank Nighbor, Harry Broadbent, Cy Denneny, Tommy Gorman (*manager*), Pete Green (*coach*).

1920/21   OTTAWA SENATORS—Jack McKell, Jack Darragh, Morley Bruce, Horace Merrill, George (Buck) Boucher, Eddie Gerard, Clint Benedict, Sprague Cleghorn, Frank Nighbor, Harry Broadbent, Cy Denneny, Tommy Gorman (*manager*), Pete Green (*coach*). C. Dolan (*trainer*).

1921/22   TORONTO ST. PATS—Ted Stackhouse, Glenn Smith, Corb Denneny, Rod Smylie, Lloyd Andrews, John Ross Roach, Harry Cameron, Red Stuart, Cecil (Babe) Dye, Ken Randall, Reg Noble, Eddie Gerard (*borrowed for the series from Ottawa*), Charlie Querrie (*manager*), Eddie Powers (*coach*).

1922/23   OTTAWA SENATORS—George (Buck) Boucher, Lionel Hitchman, Frank Nighbor, Frank (King) Clancy, Harry Helman, Clint Benedict, Jack Darragh, Eddie Gerard, Cy Denneny, Harry Broadbent, Tommy Gorman (*manager*), Pete Green (*coach*), C. Dolan (*trainer*).

1923/24   MONTREAL CANADIENS—Georges Vezina, Sprague Cleghorn, Billy Coutu, Howie Morenz, Aurel Joliat, Billy Bell, Billy Boucher, Robert Boucher, Odie Cleghorn, Sylvio Mantha, J. (Curley) Hedley, Leo Dandurand (*manager-coach*).

1924/25   VICTORIA COUGARS—Happy Holmes, Clem Loughlin, Gordie Fraser, Frank Frederickson, Jack Walker, Gizzy Hart, Slim Halderson, Frank Foyston, Harry Keeking, Jocko Anderson, Lester Patrick (*manager-coach*).

1925-26   MONTREAL MAROONS—Clint Benedict, Reg Noble, Frank Carson, Dunc Munro, Nels Stewart, Harry Broadbent, Babe Siebert, Dinny Dinsmore, Bill Phillips, Hobie Kitchen, Sammy Rothschild, Frank Lowery, Yoots Holway, Shorty Horne, Eddie Gerard (*manager-coach*), Bill O'Brien (*trainer*).

1926/27   OTTAWA SENATORS—Alex Connell, Frank (King) Clancy, George (Buck) Boucher, Ed Gorman, Frank Finnigan, Alex Smith, Hec Kilrea, Hooley Smith, Cy Denneny, Frank Nighbor, Jack Adams, Stan Jackson, Milt Halliday, Dave Gill (*manager-coach*).

1927/28   NEW YORK RANGERS—Lorne Chabot, Taffy Abel, Leo Bougault, Ching Johnson, Bill Cook, Bun Cook, Frank Boucher, Billy Boyd, Murray Murdoch, Paul Thompson, Alex Gray, Laurie Scott, Les Patrick (*sub goaltender*), Joe Miller (*sub goaltender*), Lester Patrick (*manager-coach*), Harry Westerby (*trainer*), Patsy Callighen.

1928/29   BOSTON BRUINS—Cecil (Tiny) Thompson, Hal Winkler (*sub goaltender*), Eddie Shore, Lionel Hitchman, Perk Galbraith, Eric Pettinger, Frank Frederickson, Mickey McKay, Red Green, Dutch Gainor, Harry Oliver, Eddie Rodden, Dit Clapper, Cooney Weiland, Lloyd Klein, Cy Denneny, Bill Caron, George Owen, Myles Lane, Art Ross (*manager-coach*), Win Green (*trainer*).

1929/30   MONTREAL CANADIENS—George Hainsworth, Marty Burke, Sylvio Mantha, Howie Morenz, Bert McCaffrey, Aurel Joliat, Albert Leduc, Pit Lepine, Wildor Larochelle, Nick Wasnie, Gerald Carson, Armand Mondou, George Mantha, Gus Rivers, Leo Dandurand (*manager*), Cecil Hart (*coach*), Ed Dufour (*trainer*).

1930/31   MONTREAL CANADIENS—George Hainsworth, Wildor Larochelle, Marty Burke, Sylvio Mantha, Howie Morenz, Johnny Gagnon, Aurel Joliat, Armand Mondou, Pit

Lepine, Albert Leduc, Georges Mantha, Art Lesieur, Nick Wasnie, Bert McCaffrey, Gus Rivers, Leo Dandurand (*manager*), Cecil Hart (*coach*), Ed Dufour (*trainer*).

1931/32 TORONTO MAPLE LEAFS—Chuck Conacher, Harvey Jackson, King Clancy, Andy Blair, Red Horner, Lorne Chabot, Alex Levinsky, Joe Primeau, Hal Darragh, Hal Cotton, Frank Finnigan, Hap Day, Ace Bailey, Bob Gracie, Fred Robertson, Conn Smythe (*manager*), Dick Irvin (*coach*), Tim Daly (*trainer*).

1932/33 NEW YORK RANGERS—Ching Johnson, Butch Keeling, Frank Boucher, Art Sommers, Babe Siebert, Bun Cook, Andy Aitkinhead, Ott Heller, Ozzie Asmundson, Gord Pettinger, Dough Brennan, Cecil Dillon, Bill Cook (*captain*) Murray Murdoch, Earl Seibert, Lester Patrick (*manager-coach*), Harry Westerby (*trainer*).

1933/34 CHICAGO BLACK HAWKS—Taffy Abel, Lolo Couture, Lou Trudel, Lionel Conacher, Paul Thompson, Leroy Goldsworthy, Art Coulter, Roger Jenkins, Don McFadyen, Tommy Cook, Doc Romnes, Johnny Gottselig, Mush March, Johnny Sheppard, Chuck Gardiner (*captain*), Jack Leswick, Bill Kendall, Tommy Gorman (*manager-coach*), Eddie Froelich (*trainer*).

1934/35 MONTREAL MAROONS—Marvin (Cy) Wentworth, Dutch Gainor, Alex Connell, Toe Blake, Stew Evans, Earl Robinson, Bill Miller, Dave Trottier, Jimmy Ward, Larry Northcott, Hooley Smith, Russ Blinco, Allan Shields, Sammy McManus, Gus Marker, Bob Gracie, Herb Cain, Bill MacKenzie, Tommy Gorman (*manager*), Lionel Conacher (*coach*), Bill O'Brien (*trainer*).

1935/36 DETROIT RED WINGS—Johnny Sorrell, Sid Howe, Marty Barry, Herbie Lewis, Mud Bruneteau, Wally Kilrea, Hec Kilrea, Gordon Pettinger, Bucko McDonald, Scotty Bowman, Larry Aurie, Peter Kelly, Doug Young, Ebbie Goodfellow, Normie Smith, T. Tooke (*sub goaltender*), Jack Adams (*manager-coach*), Honey Walker (*trainer*).

1936/37   DETROIT RED WINGS—Normie Smith, Pete Kelly, Larry Aurie, Herbie Lewis, Hec Kilrea, Mud Bruneteau, Sid Howe, Wally Kilrea, Jimmy Franks (*sub goaltender*), Doug Young, Bucko McDonald, Gordon Pettinger, Orville Roulston, Ebbie Goodfellow, Johnny Gallagher, Scotty Bowman, Johnny Sorrell, Marty Barry, Earl Robertson (*sub goaltender*), Johnny Sherf, Howard Mackie, Jack Adams (*manager-coach*), Honey Walker (*trainer*).

1937/38   CHICAGO BLACK HAWKS—Art Wiebe, Carl Voss, Hal Jackson, Mike Karakas, Mush March, Jack Shill, Earl Seibert, Cully Dahlstrom, Alex Levinsky, Johnny Gottsleig, Lou Trudell, Pete Palangio, Bill MacKenzie, Doc Romnes, Paul Thompson, Roger Jenkins, Virgil Johnson, Alf Moore (*sub goaltender*). Bert Connolly, Paul Goodman (*sub goaltender*), Bill Stewart (*manager-coach*), Eddie Froelich (*trainer*).

1938/39   BOSTON BRUINS—Bobby Bauer, Mel Hill, Flash Hollett, Roy Conacher, Gord Pettinger, Milt Schmidt, Woody Dumart, Jack Crawford, Ray Getliffe, Frank Brimsek, Eddie Shore, Dit Clapper, Charlie Sands, Bill Cowley, Jack Portland, Red Hamill, Art Ross (*manager-coach*), Win Green (*trainer*).

1939/40   NEW YORK RANGERS—Dave Kerr, Art Coulter, Ott Heller, Alex Shibicky, Mac Colville, Neil Colville, Phil Watson, Lynn Patrick, Clint Smith, Muzz Patrick, Babe Pratt, Bryan Hextall, Kilby Macdonald, Dutch Hiller, Alf Pike, Lester Patrick (*manager*), Frank Boucher (*coach*), Harry Westerby (*trainer*).

1940/41   BOSTON BRUINS—Bill Cowley, Des Smith, Dit Clapper, Frank Brimsek, Flash Hollett, John Crawford, Bobby Bauer, Pat McCreavy, Herb Cain, Mel Hill, Milt Schmidt, Woody Dumart, Roy Conacher, Terry Reardon, Art Jackson, Eddie Wiseman, Jack Shewchuk, Art Ross (*manager*), Cooney Weiland (*coach*), Win Green (*trainer*).

1941/42　TORONTO MAPLE LEAFS—Reg Hamilton, Wally Stanowski, Syl Apps, Bob Goldham, Gord Drillon, Hank Goldup, Ernie Dickens, Dave Schriner, Bucko McDonald, Bob Davidson, Nick Metz, Bingo Kampman, Don Metz, Gaye Stewart, Turk Broda, Johnny McCreedy, Lorne Carr, Pete Langelle, Billy Taylor, Conn Smythe (*manager*), Hap Day (*coach*), Frank Selke (*business manager*), Tim Daly (*trainer*).

1942/43　DETROIT RED WINGS—Jack Stewart, Jimmy Orlando, Sid Abel, Alex Motter, Harry Watson, Joe Carveth, Joe Turner (*sub goaltender*), Mud Bruneteau, Eddie Wares, Ralph Almas (*sub goaltender*), Johnny Mowers, Cully Simon, Don Grosso, Carl Liscombe, Connie Brown, Johnny Holota, Sid Howe, Jack Adams (*manager*), Ebbie Goodfellow (*playing-coach*), Honey Walker (*trainer*), Les Douglas, Hal Jackson, Joe Fisher.

1943/44　MONTREAL CANADIENS—Toe Blake, Maurice Richard, Elmer Lach, Ray Getliffe, Murph Chamberlain, Phil Watson, Emile Bouchard, Glen Harmon, Buddy O'Connor, Jerry Heffernan, Mike McMahon, Leo Lamoureux, Fernand Majeau, Bob Fillion, Bill Durnan, Tommy Gorman (*manager*), Dick Irvin (*coach*), Ernie Cook (*trainer*).

1944/45　TORONTO MAPLE LEAFS—Don Metz, Frank McCool, Wally Stanowski, Reg Hamilton, Elwyn Morris, Johnny McCreedy, Tommy O'Neil, Ted Kennedy, Babe Pratt, Gus Bodnar, Art Jackson, Jack McLean, Mel Hill, Nick Metz, Bob Davidson, Dave Schriner, Lorne Carr, Conn Smythe (*manager*), Frank Selke (*business manager*), Hap Day (*coach*), Tim Daly (*trainer*).

1945/46　MONTREAL CANADIENS—Elmer Lach, Toe Blake, Maurice Richard, Bob Fillion, Dutch Hiller, Murph Chamberlain, Ken Mosdell, Buddy O'Connor, Glen Harmon, Jim Peters, Emile Bouchard, Bill Reay, Ken Reardon, Leo Lamoureux, Frank Eddolls, Jerry Plamondon, Bill Durnan, Tommy Gorman (*manager*), Dick Irvin (*coach*), Ernie Cook (*trainer*).

128

1946/47   TORONTO MAPLE LEAFS—Turk Broda, Garth Boesch, Gus Mortson, Jim Thomson, Wally Stanowski, Bill Barilko, Harry Watson, Bud Poile, Ted Kennedy, Syl Apps, Don Metz, Nick Metz, Bill Ezinicki, Vic Lynn, Howie Meeker, Gaye Stewart, Joe Klukay, Gus Bodnar, Bob Goldham, Conn Smythe (*manager*), Happy Day (*coach*), Tim Daly (*trainer*).

1947/48   TORONTO MAPLE LEAFS—Turk Broda, Jim Thomson, Wally Stanowski, Garth Boesch, Bill Barilko, Gus Mortson, Phil Samis, Syl Apps, Bill Ezinicki, Harry Watson, Ted Kennedy, Howie Meeker, Vic Lynn, Nick Metz, Max Bentley, Joe Klukay, Les Costello, Don Metz, Sid Smith, Conn Smythe (*manager*), Hap Day (*coach*), Tim Daly (*trainer*).

1948/49   TORONTO MAPLE LEAFS—Turk Broda, Jim Thomson, Gus Mortson, Bill Barilko, Garth Boesch, Bill Juzda, Ted Kennedy, Howie Meeker, Vic Lynn, Harry Watson, Bill Ezinicki, Cal Gardner, Max Bentley, Joe Klukay, Sid Smith, Ray Trimgren, Don Metz, Fleming Mackell, Harry Taylor, Bob Dawes, Tod Sloan, Conn Smythe (*manager*), Hap Day (*coach*), Tim Daly (*trainer*).

1949/50   DETROIT RED WINGS—Harry Lumley, Jack Stewart, Leo Reise, Clare Martin, Al Drewsbury, Lee Fogolin, Marcel Pronovost, Red Kelly, Ted Lindsay, Sid Abel, Gordie Howe, George Gee, Jimmy Peters, Marty Pavelich, Jim McFadden, Pete Babando, Max McNab, Gerry Couture, Joe Carveth, Steve Black, John Wilson, Larry Wilson, Jack Adams (*manager*) Tommy Ivan (*coach*) Carl Mattson (*trainer*).

1950/51   TORONTO MAPLE LEAFS—Turk Broda, Al Rollins, Jim Thomson, Gus Mortson, Bill Barilko, Bill Juzda, Fern Flaman, Hugh Bolton, Ted Kennedy, Sid Smith, Tod Sloan, Cal Gardner, Howie Meeker, Harry Watson, Max Bentley, Joe Klukay, Danny Lewicki, Ray Timgren, Fleming Mackell, Johnny McCormack, Bob Hasard, Conn Smythe (*manager*), Joe Primeau (*coach*), Jim Daly (*trainer*).

1951/52   DETROIT RED WINGS—Terry Sawchuk, Bob Goldham, Ben Woit, Red Kelly, Leo Reise, Marcel Pronovost, Ted Lindsay, Tony Leswick, Gordie Howe, Metro Prystai, Marty Pavelich, Sid Abel, Glen Skov, Alex Delvecchio, Johnny Wilson, Vic Stasiuk, Larry Zeidel, Jack Adams (*manager*), Tommy Ivan (*coach*), Carl Mattson (*trainer*).

1952/53   MONTREAL CANADIENS—Gerry McNeil, Jacques Plante, Doug Harvey, Butch Bouchard, Tom Johnson, Dollard St. Laurent, Bud MacPherson, Maurice Richard, Elmer Lach, Bert Olmstead, Bernie Geoffrion, Floyd Curry, Paul Masnick, Billy Reay, Dickie Moore, Ken Mosdell, Dick Gamble, Johnny McCormack, Lorne Davis, Calum MacKay, Eddie Mazur, Frank Selke (*manager*), Dick Ivin (*coach*), Hector Dubois (*trainer*).

1953/54   DETROIT RED WINGS—Terry Sawchuk, Red Kelly, Bob Goldham, Ben Woit, Marcel Pronovost, Al Arbour, Keith Allen, Ted Lindsay, Tony Leswick, Gordie Howe, Marty Pavelich, Alex Delvecchio, Metro Prystai, Glen Skov, John Wilson, Bill Dineen, Jim Peters, Earl Reibel, Vic Stasiuk, Jack Adams (*manager*), Tommy Ivan (*coach*), Carl Mattson (*trainer*).

1954/55   DETROIT RED WINGS—Terry Sawchuk, Red Kelly, Bob Goldham, Marcel Pronovost, Ben Woit, Jim Hay, Larry Hillman, Ted Lindsay, Tony Leswick, Gordie Howe, Alex Delvecchio, Marty Pavelich, Glen Skov, Earl Reibel, John Wilson, Bill Dineen, Vic Stasiuk, Marcel Bonin, Jack Adams (*manager*), Jimmy Skinner (*coach*), Carl Mattson (*trainer*).

1955/56   MONTREAL CANADIENS—Jacques Plante, Doug Harvey, Butch Bouchard, Bob Turner, Tom Johnson, Jean-Guy Talbot, Dollard St. Laurent, Jean Beliveau, Bernie Geoffrion, Bert Olmstead, Floyd Curry, Jackie Leclair, Maurice Richard, Dickie Moore, Henri Richard, Ken Mosdell, Don Marshall, Claude Provost, Frank Selke (*manager*), Toe Blake (*coach*), Hector Dubois (*trainer*).

1956/57   MONTREAL CANADIENS—Jacques Plante, Gerry McNeil, Doug Harvey, Tom Johnson, Bob Turner, Dollard St. Laurent, Jean-Guy Talbot, Jean Beliveau, Bernie Geoffrion, Floyd Curry, Dickie Moore, Maurice Richard, Claude Provost, Bert Olmstead, Henri Richard, Phil Goyette, Don Marshall, Andre Pronovost, Connie Broden, Frank Selke (*manager*), Toe Blake (*coach*), Hector Dubois (*trainer*).

1957/58   MONTREAL CANADIENS—Jacques Plante, Gerry McNeil, Doug Harvey, Tom Johnson, Bob Turner, Dollard St. Laurent, Jean-Guy Talbot, Albert Langlois, Jean Beliveau, Bernie Geoffrion, Maurice Richard, Dickie Moore, Claude Provost, Bert Olmstead, Henri Richard, Marcel Bonin, Phil Goyette, Don Marshall, André Pronovost, Connie Broden, Frank Selke (*manager*), Toe Blake (*coach*), Hector Dubois (*trainer*).

1958/59   MONTREAL CANADIENS—Jacques Plante, Charlie Hodge, Doug Harvey, Tom Johnson, Bob Turner, Jean-Guy Talbot, Albert Langlois, Jean Beliveau, Bernie Geoffrion, Ralph Backstrom, Bill Hicke, Maurice Richard, Dickie Moore, Claude Provost, Ab McDonald, Henri Richard, Marcel Bonin, Phil Goyette, Don Marshall, Marcel Pronovost, Frank Selke (*manager*), Toe Blake (*coach*), Hector Dubois (*trainer*).

1959/60   MONTREAL CANADIENS—Jacques Plante, Charlie Hodge, Doug Harvey, Tom Johnson, Bob Turner, Jean-Guy Talbot, Albert Langlois, Ralph Backstrom, Jean Beliveau, Marcel Bonin, Bernie Geoffrion, Phil Goyette, Bill Hicke, Don Marshall, Ab McDonald, Dickie Moore, André Pronovost, Claude Provost, Henri Richard, Maurice Richard, Frank Selke (*manager*), Toe Blake (*coach*), Hector Dubois, Larry Aubut (*trainers*).

1960/61   CHICAGO BLACK HAWKS—Glenn Hall, Al Arbour, Pierre Pilote, Elmer Vasko, Jack Evans, Dollard St. Laurent, Reg Fleming, Tod Sloan, Ron Murphy, Eddie Litzenberger, Bill Hay, Bobby Hull, Ab McDonald, Eric Nesterenko, Ken Wharram, Earl Balfour, Stan Mikita, Murray Balfour, Tommy Ivan (*manager*), Rudy Pilous (*coach*), Nick Garen (*trainer*).

1961/62   TORONTO MAPLE LEAFS—Johnny Bower, Don Simmons, Carl Brewer, Tim Horton, Bob Baun, Allan Stanley, Al Arbour, Larry Hillman, Red Kelly, Dick Duff, George Armstrong, Frank Mahovlich; Bob Nevin, Ron Stewart, Billy Harris, Bert Olmstead, Bob Pulford, Eddie Shack, Dave Keon, Ed Litzenberger, John MacMillan, Punch Imlach (*manager-coach*), Bob Haggert (*Trainer*).

1962/63   TORONTO MAPLE LEAFS—Johnny Bower, Don Simmons, Carl Brewer; Tim Horton, Bob Baun, Kent Douglas, Allan Stanley, Red Kelly, Dick Duff, George Armstrong, Frank Mahovlich, Bob Nevin, Ron Stewart, Dave Keon, Billy Harris, Bob Pulford, Eddie Shack, Ed Litzenberger, John MacMillan; Larry Hillman, Punch Imlach (*manager-coach*), Bob Haggert (*trainer*).